SIMPLE NUMBERS,

STRAIGHT TALK,

BIG

4 KEYS TO UNLOCK YOUR BUSINESS POTENTIAL

PROFITS!

SIMPLE NUMBERS, STRAIGHT TALK, BIG PROFITS!

4 KEYS TO UNLOCK YOUR BUSINESS POTENTIAL

GREG CRABTREE

WITH BEVERLY BLAIR HARZOG

MJ Lane
Publishing

Published by MJ Lane Publishing
Huntsville, Alabama

For ordering information or special discounts for bulk purchases, please contact
MJ Lane Publishing, 3626 Memorial Parkway, SW, Huntsville, AL 35801, 256.704.0620.

Design and composition by Greenleaf Book Group LLC and Alex Head
Cover design by Greenleaf Book Group LLC

Publisher's Cataloging-In-Publication Data
(Prepared by The Donohue Group, Inc.)
Crabtree, Greg (Gregory Burges), 1957-
  Simple numbers, straight talk, big profits! : 4 keys to unlock your business potential / Greg
Crabtree ; with Beverly Blair Harzog. — 1st ed.
  p. ; cm.
  ISBN: 978-0-9896452-2-5
  1. Small business—Finance—Handbooks, manuals, etc. 2. Small business—Accounting—
Handbooks, Manuals, etc. 3. Success in business. I. Harzog, Beverly Blair. II. Title.
HG4027.7 .C72 2011
658.159/2   2011923304

Printed in the United States of America

15 16 17 18 19 10 9 8 7 6 5 4

First Edition

CONTENTS

FOREWORD

Save yourself a million dollars and read Greg's book.

When I launched my business, I grew it from $500,000 to $1 million to $2 million to what was supposed to be $4 million in revenue in 2001; then 9/11 hit and I was days from losing my business (and our family's home). Not only had I lost a million dollars within eight weeks, all along the way I was dutifully losing money each year—money five of my friends had loaned me—and justifying the losses because I was "investing" in the growth of my business.

It was then that I became serious about paying myself, improving my margins, and paying back my investors. The first thing I did was heed the advice of my advisors, who kept warning me that my gross margin was too low. So my critical number for 2002 was to raise my gross margin from 43 percent to 55 percent. I also started having my accountant report my cash position to me each day.

Through a lot of hard work and focus, my team and I did it. And with the increased gross margin came our first profitable year ever, helping me generate enough cash to repay my investors and make good money ever since.

In this book, Greg has distilled key lessons for making serious money in your business—lessons I had to learn the hard and painful way. One warning: he doesn't add a lot of fluff to his points. He tells it like it is, starting with the first page. More importantly, he highlights some truths about business I've yet to see articulated in any other book on growing a business, starting with the fatal mistake of thinking you're making a great profit without accounting for a reasonable salary for yourself.

I've known Greg for many years, first as a student of mine in the Entrepreneurs' Organization's Advanced Business executive program at MIT and today as a colleague and friend who helps firms navigate the challenges of growing a business.

Greg also gives his time to the Accelerator initiative in the Entrepreneurs' Organization to help firms under $1 million in revenue obtain the necessary escape velocity to surpass the $1 million mark and join the Entrepreneurs' Organization. And his tips are universal for much, much larger companies.

Greg has helped hundreds of companies, and he can help yours. He's that rare accountant who can see beyond the numbers. Tap into his wealth of experience and put it to work in your business.

Verne Harnish,
Founder, Entrepreneurs' Organization
September 11, 2010

INTRODUCTION

I can only dream as far as I can see . . .
And when I get there, I can always see farther.

—Anonymous

Every business starts with a seed of an idea, but only a few entrepreneurs can visualize the field all the way through harvest, much less through many successive seasons. By seeing beyond the numbers, I have laid out the basic principles that can help entrepreneurs create a realistic vision of their business from the beginning through many bountiful harvests.

I will share my experience on how to lay a solid foundation to build and manage your business, which is based on hundreds of real businesses, not cocktail party advice. We start with your dual role of key employee *and* shareholder and how something so seemingly simple can mess up so many businesses. We then move to learning the connections among profits, cash flow, and the productivity of labor.

If you feel that your business is sucking the life out of you, you'll learn why the black hole phase of business exists and how you can get beyond it to smoother sailing. With profitability comes taxes, and I will show you how to fearlessly face the tax monster under your bed. Once you get the broken parts of your business fixed, you need a monitoring system that is simple and constantly pulses the right data at the right time. At this point, you'll understand the economic value of your business and have a clear vision of whether you should offer stock to partners or employees, sell the business, or keep it healthy and harvest the profits to build your own wealth.

This book is primarily aimed at business owners from startup to $5 million in revenue. However, you should read this book before you even start a business. Many of my peers in the Entrepreneurs' Organization who have a business with revenue beyond $5 million have found the concepts clarifying and valuable.

I come by the farming references honestly because I was raised on a chicken farm in Northeast Alabama and learned at an early age what I did not want to do for a living! I was fortunate to have worked for great mentors in both public accounting and a bank before I started my own CPA firm, where I focused on helping entrepreneurs see beyond numbers.

After becoming a member of the Entrepreneurs' Organization in 2001, I became connected with entrepreneurs from around the world who communicate by sharing experiences instead of theory. As I grew my firm, I learned that sharing stories was a far superior method of communicating how to build a better entrepreneur. It also allowed me to develop and grow my team of new college graduates and fill their heads with fresh ideas without having them unlearn baggage that might hold them back.

I get to see intimate data from hundreds of businesses that are the basis for the stories and ideas included in this book. I have changed the names and details to protect their identity, but not enough to change the meaning of the data.

This material was developed from the sessions I have taught for the Entrepreneurs' Organization chapter learning events and their Accelerator Program for businesses that are not yet large enough to join the Entrepreneurs' Organization. It is my hope that this book helps you dream farther because you can see farther!

SECTION 1: THE FOUR KEYS

The four chapters in this section outline the solutions to the main recurring problems I see in businesses that are between startup and $5 million in revenue. It is important to review these chapters in sequence since the concepts build on each other.

You must get owner compensation right to know what your true pretax profit is. Once you know your true profit, you can set your sights on the correct target.

When you know what you are aiming for, you must establish an understanding of how to manage labor productivity to meet your goals. As you become more profitable, prioritization of your cash flow becomes a strategic endeavor instead of a fire drill with no exits.

Anyone can understand these concepts, regardless of their understanding of finances or their educational background. Most of these ideas came from studying successful entrepreneurs who have never gone to college, much less taken an accounting class.

Above all, keep it simple!

CHAPTER 1

OWNER'S SALARY: WHY YOUR SALARY AND DISTRIBUTIONS ARE FOGGING YOUR VIEW OF NET INCOME

It's my company—why can't I pay myself whatever I please?

I've always felt that accountants make finances too hard to understand. In my practice, we look at numbers in a simplified way and use entrepreneur speak to simplify the concepts. This seems natural since we're entrepreneurs ourselves.

When I started brainstorming for this book, I was stunned when I realized that I had never seen my first key topic discussed in any book about entrepreneurial success. That topic is the owner's salary. It's a tremendously important concept, but entrepreneurs often misunderstand the relationship between their salary and the return on what they own. In fact, all of my clients have confused the profits of their business with their salary. Remember this key distinction: You get paid a salary for what you do, and you get a return on what you own.

Why is this so important? Because when you don't pay yourself a market-based wage, your net income number is lying to you. Or rather, you are lying to yourself. Until you pay yourself a market-based wage and plug that number into your financials (a number that's reasonable—not too high or too low), your financial data is worthless. It's like having a compass that's five degrees off in every direction. If you don't include a realistic wage for yourself in your financials, your business will always head in the wrong direction.

Deciding on an appropriate wage for yourself is really a key building block for your business. As we'll see, it will help clarify a lot of other issues. But don't just take my word for it. Occasionally, I'll use actual questions and answers from the entrepreneur classes I teach to illustrate key points, like the following exchange:

> Entrepreneur: *Can you give me an example of how paying yourself a below-market salary distorts financial numbers?*
>
> Greg: *A great example involves one of my clients. They are a couple and co-owners in a business. They were patting themselves on the back because they were making a net income that was more than 20 percent of sales. Or at least they thought they were. Unfortunately they were paying themselves a very small salary and taking distributions out of the business. After I added their salaries and distributions together and treated this number as if it were a true market-based wage, they were actually only making 5 percent before taxes.*

This happens constantly in businesses. Most entrepreneurs think they are overpaying themselves, but at least 90 percent are *underpaying* themselves. I think this is common because entrepreneurs want to show off their peacock feathers in public, and they use sales numbers and net income for their first extravagant display. But sales figures and net income are irrelevant if business owners don't include a true market-based wage in their financials. As the old saying goes, "Sales are for show, profits are for dough!" That's why so much of the data in the marketplace—whether it is industry data or comparative data among other industries—is worthless. Until you apply the market-based wage filter across that data, none of it is relevant.

If you've been in business for yourself for a long time, you receive a Social Security wage statement either once a year or every two years (depending on your age). Look at that statement, because it tells you what your W2 earnings totals have been over time and what your estimated Social Security payments will be when you retire. This can be a very sobering thing if you decided that you would make low wages and distribute the profits of the business to yourself.

KEEPING UNCLE SAM HAPPY MAY BE YOUR BEST KEY INDICATOR

No one wants to mess with the IRS. When you don't pay yourself a market-based wage, your financials are distorted, and the IRS takes notice. How is that?

For example, if your company is an S corporation, it's a bad plan to pay low wages to avoid payroll taxes. This practice is on the IRS's list of Dirty Dozen tax scams, and they look for it when they review your tax return. If you pay yourself wages that are too low, you run a high risk of an IRS audit. During the past two years they've audited the returns of thirty thousand S corporations based on this one issue.

I understand that everyone hates to pay taxes. Too often people use taxes as their excuse for bad performance and say, "I made money, but then I had to pay it all in taxes." Even if they are making money, some business owners will do anything to avoid paying money to the IRS, even if it hurts their business.

There is never a case in which the entire next dollar of profit goes to taxes. The top federal tax bracket is 35 percent, so you keep 65 cents on every dollar (before state taxes), and that's a lot better than nothing. If your company is an LLC, all of your profits are subject to employment taxes so the IRS does not care how much you take in salary or distributions. But if your company is an S corporation, this is a red flag because the IRS will say the distributions should be salary. Either way, you're taking income out of the business and decreasing profits that need to be left in the business to keep it healthy.

One thing I say to my clients all the time is that if you're not paying taxes, there are only two possibilities: You didn't make any income or you're cheating. Paying taxes is a good thing. The higher your tax bill, the better your business is doing. This is your number one key performance indicator. You can't create legitimate wealth from an operating business unless you pay taxes. Your business's number one key performance indicator is this: *How big a check did you write to the IRS this year?* If you're my client and I've done my job, I can show you how much more money you made even though you paid taxes. I have clients who paid $1 million in taxes, and I was able to show them that they still kept $2 million. A million-dollar tax bill is no fun, but these clients created true wealth that could be traced to real money in the bank. Beware of people who promise to lower your tax bill to 10 percent or less. They are using the *effective tax rate* as a lure to have you spend all your profits to lower your tax bill. The effective tax rate refers to the amount of tax you paid divided by your total income before deductions. Beware when people explain taxes this way, because they are luring you into spending money on deductions as a way to lower your tax bill. You will pay less in taxes, but you will never build any wealth.

This is probably different from what you're used to hearing from most accountants because they tell you how to save on taxes. But if I'm saving you taxes because you spent your profit, am I really saving you anything? Don't focus so hard on not paying taxes. Focus instead on increasing your profits. Of course, you have to plan carefully for taxes when you pay yourself a market-based wage. I'll talk about this in more detail in chapter 5, "Taming the Tax Monster Under Your Bed: Tax Management That Works."

DETERMINING A MARKET-BASED WAGE

You have to determine your market-based wage before you can plug it into your financials. One of the greatest quotes I've ever heard is, "A man who aims at nothing hits it with amazing accuracy." I'll help you figure out how to take aim with your salary calculation and hit the target.

As I go from city to city talking to entrepreneurs, I encounter an amazing consensus that $30,000 is the acceptable owner's salary. Why is $30,000 the magic number? I have no idea, but it is far too low for the vast majority of business owners. One of my clients was paying himself a $30,000 salary and taking large distributions. I recognized this as a problem and immediately advised him to change his pay. A short time later, he received notice from the IRS that he was being audited for unreasonable compensation. This salary doesn't fly unless you really are doing a job that's worth only $30,000, in which case you'd better have some salary surveys to prove it. This situation can become very expensive if you end up having to deal with the IRS. And if your job is worth only $30,000, why are you doing it? No entrepreneurs I know truly believe their work is worth only $30,000.

Determining what your salary should be is confusing to many entrepreneurs. Here's a common question I hear:

> Entrepreneur: *You said $30,000 is kind of a magic number. If I'm paying myself that wage now, how do I determine if it really should be higher?*

> Greg: *Think of it like this: If you got run over by a bus today and your heirs decided they would keep the business going in your absence, what would they have to pay someone to do your job?*

There are plenty of salary survey websites. Some of the numbers might be overinflated, even if you knock them back 10 to 20 percent. But even after adjusting them, it's likely that the numbers will still be significantly higher than what you're paying yourself today. My practice subscribes to the Economic Research Institute's Salary Survey Assessor (www.erieri.com). It is one of the main salary survey sites, and it's the engine for most salary surveys. I've always been able to find a relevant salary survey to give clients some direction without much difficulty. Another website to check out is Salary.com. We'll discuss other ways to determine your market-based wage in chapter 6, "How to Maximize Your Labor Productivity."

Because my practice has worked with so many companies in so many industries, we have a pretty good idea of what a CEO should get paid. If you're doing $1 million in revenue, it's unlikely that you'll make $200,000 as the CEO. We typically look at ranges to determine a CEO's salary. You probably have one or two people in four or five key functional roles in your business, so you should take a blended approach to setting salary levels. A great example of this is a business where the CEO is also responsible for sales. The CEO function of a business with $1 million of revenue is not a full-time role and accounts for only 20 percent of the owner's time. The remainder of the owner's time is spent on sales. If the owner takes a salary of $125,000 per year, $25,000 is the CEO salary, and $100,000 is the VP of sales salary. You can see the problem that arises when the CEO decides to hire a VP of sales. The CEO would have to take a salary cut. The solution is that the CEO continues to sell along with the VP of sales, and the business grows faster so it can eventually justify a full-time CEO. In a single-shareholder business, there are times when the shareholder can decide not to take a market-based wage and remain within the IRS guidelines of reasonable pay. But I still believe the profit card should always trump a tax strategy.

A BUSINESS IS LIKE A COW

Most people know they've actively avoided the issue of paying themselves a market-based wage. But increasing their pay sometimes leads to another question: I really should be making $100,000, but what should I do if I can only *afford* to pay myself $30,000? If you're not able to pay yourself a market-based wage so you can see the true metrics of your business, you're operating at a loss. You can't let this phase go on too long because you will eventually face two bad scenarios: a below-market wage and no return on your investment. You need to devise a plan that will deliver you a market-based salary and a good return on your investment.

In the next chapter, I'll talk about how to fix an underperforming business. But for now, it's important to understand that if you are under-paying yourself, your business is sick. I like to say that a business is like a cow. Until you pay yourself a market-based wage—and make a profit on top of that—you have a sick cow on your hands. Your goal is to keep the cow healthy so you can milk it every day. Or you can have one barbecue. Take your pick. In other words, your goal should be to create a business that generates income for you every day rather than killing your business by taking out too much income at one time. But don't worry—I'll show you how to keep your business (your cash cow) healthy.

SWEAT EQUITY

You shouldn't pay yourself a market-based salary when your business can't afford it. There's a different way to pay yourself what you are worth without taking cash out of the business. It's called *sweat equity*.

Sweat equity is the value you have created for your business through your unpaid work. If your business should be paying you $100,000 per year for the job you perform in your business, and it takes you two years before you can draw your salary, you have just created $200,000 in capital through sweat equity. This is a very important concept, whether you have outside investors or not, because it lets you calculate your lost opportunity to earn market-based wages had you chosen to work else-where. If you have outside investors, it gives you a way to balance the worth of your effort with the money they invested. Either way, it's a great opportunity to understand the difference between "I'm still putting in sweat equity and I'm not going to stop until I get my full salary" and "I've made an acceptable profit above my salary by calculating my real sweat equity!"

You can track your sweat equity and make an adjustment when it comes time to do your tax return so it doesn't distort your numbers. Or you can calculate it separately in your financial performance metrics. I've found that most accounting systems really struggle to give you the finan-cial reporting you need for special items like tracking sweat equity. Most of the time, you need to take data from an accounting system and put it in a format that makes it readable. You'll find some examples on my website, www.seeingbeyondnumbers.com.

MARKET-BASED WAGES FOR ALL

Now is a good time to talk about market forces in relation to this question:

> Entrepreneur: *Does the market-based wage apply only to you as a shareholder, or does it apply to affiliates as well?*
>
> Greg: *Market-based wages apply to everybody, not just the shareholder.*

If I hire an employee at below-market rate, market forces dictate that I'm not going to keep that person forever, and replacement will be more costly in the long run than hiring that employee at the market rate. A high turnover rate is very, very expensive. It also makes it hard to create consistency in the workplace, which can lower productivity, service quality, and customer satisfaction (this is also expensive). If you're a multi-shareholder company, market-based wages can become a real issue. Here's a scenario I've seen many times. Three guys have been buddies forever, and they're ready to start a business:

> First buddy: *Okay, there are three of us starting this business.*
>
> Greg: *Sounds great. What's the ownership going to be?*
>
> Second buddy: *Oh, it's one-third each.*
>
> Greg: *Really? Is everybody going to put in the same amount of money?*
>
> Third buddy: *Well, two of us are going to put in a little bit of money, but Bob's not going to put in any money.*

But we really need him to be part of the business.

Greg: *So what's the compensation structure?*

All the buddies: *We're all going to make the same salary.*

Greg: *Really? I have news for you: fair does not mean equal.*

I've rarely seen two people worth exactly the same amount of money. I've never seen three people worth the same amount of money. A lot of people find themselves in this situation, and they ask me how to fix it. I tell them they need to have an honest and frank discussion. A lot of times, I mediate these situations, or if there's somebody else in the business who is respected by all the parties, that person will mediate. The people who have this discussion in the early stages of business formation are the ones who succeed. The CEO should usually be the highest paid salaried employee in the business. There are only two positions that might get a higher salary than the CEO. One is a salesperson who's on an eat-what-you-kill incentive program. The other is an expert technical person who gets a high salary at the early stage of the business when you have to build the whole business off of that person's technical skill set. You might give the technical expert some ownership just for the sake of it, but you're really leveraging that person's technical ability with your ability to be an entrepreneur. When you have just one technical person who is an expert (and not the CEO) the business is not vibrant enough to pay the CEO more than the expert. Once you have multiple experts on staff and support people, the CEO has a much larger enterprise and can justify the largest salary.

There is another major problem with three friends setting up a business and proposing to be paid an equal salary. No one is the leader. Management by committee is an absolute failure as a business model. *There has to be a clear leader even if the stock ownership is equal.* If no one is seen as the clear leader and director of the business, it will stagnate very quickly because you won't have a focused leader saying, "Here's the way forward. You guys follow me!" You may want to answer salary and leadership questions over a period of time, but you need to make these tough decisions within a couple of years. The success of your business depends on it. Sometimes multiple shareholders have different needs when it comes to salaries. Here's another common scenario:

> Entrepreneur: *I have a partner and only one of us is taking home a salary because my partner can afford not to. What do we do about straightening out this problem?*

> Greg: *When you're in a situation where you've got two shareholders and there's not enough profit for everybody to make a market-based wage, you need to account for it as debt as the unpaid salary builds up or as an accrued salary that wasn't paid. If you don't use either of these approaches, there has to be a shift in equity ownership.*

I like the sweat equity solution. Maybe you do it in two phases. You start out with a debt up to a predetermined point, and when the debt reaches that point, you make some equity changes. I've done this in my own business when some of the partners couldn't go without compensation. We adjusted the equity based on who could go without a wage and who couldn't.

GOT INVESTORS? QUANTIFY EVERYTHING

Sometimes having an outside investor makes owners think twice about paying themselves a market-based salary:

> Entrepreneur: *I have a multi-shareholder company in which I'm the employee shareholder and I have an outside investor. The investor isn't being paid, of course, since he's only an investor. But how do I get the investor to understand that I need to be paid fairly for what I do?*

Greg: *One of the best examples is when you have what I call a money partner (the owner who provides investment capital to the business) and an effort partner (the owner who works in the business but does not have money to invest in the business). If I'm starting a business with you and I have the ability to do something but I have no cash, I need a funder to put money in. This philosophy says that 100 percent of the profits and losses of the business should be allocated to the money partner until that partner recoups the initial investment. After that, you move to some agreed profit-and-loss percentage.*

Let's say I'm worth $100,000, but I'm going to take only a $30,000 salary. This way, I pay back my money partners $70,000 a year sooner than if I had taken my full salary. This is a phenomenally effective way for you to create capital in the business. The key, though, is to never let yourself be trapped into thinking that you're worth only $30,000 a year. Make sure that you will be able to move your salary to a market-based wage at some point. You must discuss the wage issue with the money partner up front. Decide what the market-based wage is from the very start so you're in agreement when the time comes to increase your salary.

If you can't go without a market-based wage, it means that your standard of living requires you to be paid your full salary from the beginning. In this case, you're going to slow the process of the investor getting back the return on his or her investment. I'm not a fan of sharing profits before the investors are paid back. There's always going to be some animosity. The investor will think: *Hey, I put all the money in, and you're getting your salary and a share of the profits. Look at how long it will take for me to get my money back.*

One of the skill sets that we've built into our firm is the ability to forecast and quantify every situation. We believe that you have to play out multiple scenarios—actually plan out those cash flows—and create reasonable expectations for the investor. Will it take eighteen months for the investors to get their money back? Or will it take five years? And is there a scenario in which an investor never gets the money? If that last question is a possibility, the deal shouldn't have been done! Quantify everything, and put it in writing.

TRANSITIONING OUT OF YOUR BUSINESS

Here's another way in which giving yourself a market-based wage helps you. Let's say you're the founder of a business, a single shareholder, and you're ready to sell the business or transition out of it. If you're not paying yourself a market-based wage, you really don't know what it means from a financial standpoint to bring in another general manager. You'll have to pay your replacement a market-based wage, and this will negatively impact your business's net income. But if you're already paying yourself a market-based wage, it's easier to step out of the role of being an active manager and into the role of being only a shareholder. You can hire your replacement with no negative impact on your net income. Not only that, you have a methodology in place that reflects the true profitability of your business.

Instead of retiring, you might consider a part-time role that pays less than your CEO salary, such as being a finance person or a customer advocate. I recommend easing out slowly, because stepping out of a business abruptly usually creates a vacuum. This approach allows you to effectively transition out of the business in phases. You'll also know if your business will produce, for example, $500,000 a year of pretax profit no matter who's running it. And if you give your replacement a market-based wage while you stay on in a lesser role, then you can hold that new person accountable.

You can even set up an incentive program to motivate the new CEO. Tell the new person, "I'll share a percentage of anything you get above my baseline profit number. Your baseline could be what the business was doing before you hired on as the new CEO or it could even be a higher target. But if you don't get what I was getting when I was CEO, you'd better give me a good reason. Is the market causing lower revenue and profitability, or is it because you can't make it happen?"

This naturally leads to a question:

> Entrepreneur: *So how do I know what my business's baseline number should be?*
>
> Greg: *There are some business performance basics that help you decide your target profitability level. And then you've got to adjust salaries and all the other operating expenses to make sure that you hit those profitability levels.*

In the next few chapters, we'll touch on these business performance basics, and I'll show you how to build your business up from your baseline number. It's not as complex as everybody likes to make it seem.

TWO CHALLENGES

Are you underpaying yourself and bragging about your sales or your net income? To make sure you are not just showing off your peacock feathers when you talk about your financials, you need to face two challenges.

Challenge #1: Be a More Demanding Employee

Are you making $30,000 a year when you're really worth $100,000, or maybe even $150,000 or $200,000 a year? If so, why are you willing to work for such a low salary? To answer this question, you need a long-term goal that makes working for such a low salary worth your while, and you need a plan to pay yourself a market-based salary after that goal is met—a real cash salary, not a distribution of profits.

Challenge #2: Be a Demanding Shareholder

If you are accepting a below-market wage, you are overstating the profits of your business. As a demanding shareholder, you would never stand for that.

If you're a single-shareholder business and you can't be demanding enough on your own, you may need to have a one-on-one relationship with a key advisor. If your advisor is not really helping, it's okay to end the relationship. Find a different advisor who will talk straight and help you drive your business forward.

I've had clients who have used advisory boards, which were usually found largely ineffective. If you chose to have an advisory board, make sure you aren't listening to too many voices, and make sure the voices you are listening to have something relevant to say.

Keep your goal in mind: You don't want your numbers to lie to you. Inaccurate numbers will distort your financial information and cause other problems as well.

Chapter 1 Keys

1. Know what your market-based wage is for your role. If the business cannot afford to pay you, keep track of the wages you are giving up.

2. If you are profitable and you pay yourself wages that are too low, you run a high risk of an IRS audit. And no one wants an IRS audit.

3. Value profitability over tax savings. Stop distorting your net income because of improper owner compensation.

4. Use market-based wages for everyone in the business, including shareholders.

5. Pay back your investors before you share profits, and create reasonable financial expectations for your investors.

6. Consider working in a limited capacity at a lower wage as you transition out of active management.

CHAPTER 2

PROFIT: WHY 10 PERCENT IS THE NEW BREAKEVEN

Profit is like oxygen—your business can't hold its breath very long without it.

You know that you have to pay yourself a market-based wage and get a return on what you own. If you're not at the point where you can do this, then you're not profitable enough. Maybe you're thinking, "I'm committed to my business, and I want to pay myself a market-based wage for the things I do. But I'm not getting enough profit out of the business to be able to do that." How do you fix that problem?

THE IMPORTANCE OF PRETAX PROFIT

First you have to understand the concept of profit. Profit is the lifeblood of every business. If your business isn't profitable, you're taking business from others and you will eventually fade away. You either have to be profitable or have an endless amount of capital to throw at your business. To keep it simple, when I say *profit*, I'm talking about pretax profit. This is the profit you make after you take all your sales minus all your costs, before you pay taxes.

If you can't pay yourself a market-based wage, the first thing to focus on is getting your business profitable. Remember the cow analogy in chapter 1? You can keep your cow healthy and milk it every day, or you can have one big barbecue dinner. Think of the milk as profit. It eventually turns into cash flow, but you have to be profitable first.

A lot of business books and articles use the term *EBITDA*, which means earnings before interest, taxes, depreciation, and amortization. There's a game, largely played in the investment banking community, where they recast earnings and say that interest, depreciation, and amortization aren't real costs. But let's face it. Unless you're building a twenty-year production plant that is going to last fifty years, depreciation is a real cost. If you buy a truck for $50,000 and it wears out in five years, you'll have to replace it. That's a real cost. Amortization is just a fancy term that spreads the cost of nonequipment over years just like depreciation, but very few entrepreneurs deal with amortized costs that are significant.

Technically, interest is not an operating cost. Generally accepted accounting principles (GAAP) are great, but at the end of the day, entrepreneurs need to be practical. When you write a check for interest, you have to pay real money to cover that check. It takes cash out of your business and typically indicates your business is undercapitalized. This is an important aspect of interest, and it's the key reason I focus on pretax profit.

Pretax profit is your earnings before taxes. That is the revenue-generating activity that your business produces for your benefit. In most of the businesses I work with, interest, depreciation, and amortization are real numbers, so it's important to understand that you should ignore EBITDA and focus on your pretax profit.

As I said in chapter 1, revenue is for show, and profit is for dough. I couldn't care less how much revenue you have. It's an important number in terms of cash turnover, but we need to focus primarily on your gross profit before we can fix your pretax profit. Gross profit is revenue less cost of goods sold. Contrary to many other accountants, I recommend that you not include any labor costs in getting to gross profit. By keeping labor out of the equation, my definition of gross profit gets you to the number that is the true economic engine of the business.

Cost of goods sold typically includes pass-through costs like finished goods, materials, and subcontractors. These costs will vary dramatically among businesses and industries. By focusing on gross profit instead of revenue, most businesses from any industry can be compared side to side. For instance, I can take a service-based business and compare it to a retailer, and then I can compare the retailer to a building contractor. I can compare the building contractor to a government contractor because when I sell materials, I'm really selling the services of the people who deliver the materials. If I have labor that I want to account for as direct labor (that is, labor that is directly responsible for product or service delivery), I show it on a separate line below gross profit. Gross profit minus your direct labor is then what I refer to as your contribution margin before you pay for your general operating expenses. Don't think of subcontractors as your labor that you make money from. If I hire a subcontractor, I have to leave profit in the equation for the subcontractor's business since I am offloading my downtime risk to the subcontractor. Therefore, I am just passing through some of my revenue to the subcontractor. You can show the world all the expanded financials you want, but you have to come back to reality and filter out the cost of goods sold.

If a construction contractor has a $20 million business, that's great. But by the time he subtracts what he pays for subcontractors and materials, he probably has a $2 million or $3 million business that looks like any other service-based business. That's why your revenue doesn't matter. Your gross profit matters most, followed by how you get to pretax profit.

Take a look at exhibit 2.1. It compares a construction contractor with a services business. There is a dramatic difference in their revenue and cost of goods sold, but starting with the gross profit line, they are exactly the same. The construction company survives on less pretax profit as a percentage of revenue because they try to not pay their subcontractors and material vendors until they get paid. It is as if they are a selling agent for the materials and their subcontractors.

Exhibit 2.1: Gross Profit Examples		
	Construction Company	Services Company
Revenue	$20,000,000	$3,750,000
Cost of Goods Sold:		
Materials	5,000,000	-
Subcontractors	12,150,000	900,000
Total Cost of Goods Sold	17,150,000	900,000
Gross Profit	2,850,000	2,850,000
Direct Labor	1,000,000	1,000,000
Contribution Margin	1,850,000	1,850,000
Operating expenses:		
Facilities	150,000	150,000
Marketing	75,000	75,000
Salaries (management and admin)	750,000	750,000
Payroll taxes and benefits	100,000	100,000
Other operating expenses	150,000	150,000
Net Operating Income	625,000	625,000
Other expenses:		
Depreciation	75,000	75,000
Interest Expense	25,000	25,000
Total other expenses	100,000	100,000
Pretax Profit	$525,000	$525,000
as a % of Revenue	2.63%	14.00%
as a % of Gross Profit	18.42%	18.42%

Entrepreneur: *So are you basically saying I was doing things that I wasn't admitting to myself that I was doing? But I could get away with it because I was small?*

Greg: *That's right. There's a little bit of business snobbery that goes on because everybody loves this revenue thing. I'm more proud of a business owner who gets a million dollars of revenue and brings home a half-million dollars in profit than someone who's earning $5 million dollars in revenue but is in debt up to the eyeballs. He can't even pay himself a salary, and he's about to go broke.*

BREAKING EVEN ISN'T GOOD ENOUGH

Every business owner who's either starting a business or running a business probably instinctively knows what the breakeven point means. The standard definition is when the business has income that equals its expenses. At my firm, we discovered that the breakeven concept is a flawed way of thinking. By the time you're at the breakeven point, your business is already dead.

After we looked at breakeven analyses, we concluded that when your pretax profit is at or below 5 percent of revenue, your business is on life support. At that point, you've got to do something drastic. When it comes to pretax profit, here's what I've found to be true for the vast majority of businesses:

- 5 percent or less of pretax profit means your business is on life support.
- 10 percent of pretax profit means you have a good business.
- 15 percent or more of pretax profit means you have a *great* business.

If you're above 15 percent, you better take it while you can because the market will eventually change. The best businesses tend to operate between 10 percent and 15 percent.

After businesses get beyond $5 million, there are a few outliers. For example, grocery stores have a very low margin and high turnover of goods. Distribution businesses may earn $40 million a year in revenue but only have a 5 percent bottom line. They have very low margins and usually don't have to pay for what they sell until they collect it from their customers, so they have back-to-back financing.

When you first start a business, you're just happy to get your salary, and then you're happy to reach the breakeven point. Later you're happy to have a little bit of profit. I frequently see entrepreneurs who become ecstatic over that first bit of profit. Then a nasty little realization pops into their heads: *I owe taxes on that*. But that's not a bad thing. Remember from chapter 1 that your number one key performance indicator is how big a check you write to the IRS.

THE EIGHT FUNCTIONAL AREAS

There's a natural differential that takes place between startup and hitting the $1 million-in-revenue mark. This is probably contrary to what many others think, but I believe that once you get to a million dollars of revenue, you'd better be profitable and paying yourself a market-based wage. Keep in mind that a market-based wage is based on what your role is. If you were an executive making a $150,000 a year but now you're a store manager for Fred's Lawn Care, your market-based wage isn't $150,000 anymore.

What happens at a million dollars is that you can no longer take care of all the functional positions. You need enough revenue to cover the costs of paying market wages for people to perform in all of your business's functional positions. If you can't cover these costs with your million dollars in revenue, you are not making a profit, and you will quickly go out of business. One of the things I do when I sit down with owners of million-dollar businesses is ask them to put the responsible person's name beside these eight functional areas:

1. CEO: In most cases, the CEO is the owner, but you may want to hire one if you are not the best fit.

2. Sales: Sales management is the key function, more so than who actually does the selling.

3. Marketing: I make a distinct differentiation between sales and

marketing; they are two different functional areas. The same person may be doing both jobs, but they're not the same job.

4. Operations: This is the person who makes sure that the trains run on time and that whatever product or service you're selling gets delivered.

5. IT and technology development: You need somebody to take care of information technology capabilities. These days, everybody needs some IT in their cupboard. You might outsource it, but somebody needs to own that function.

6. Finance: Somebody has to pay the bills, balance the checkbook, and do basic financial reporting. You can outsource part of it, but someone in the company has to be responsible for it.

7. Customer service: Who's the customer service advocate? There is an overlap between sales and operations in meeting your customer expectations. Someone needs to bridge these two areas to make sure the customer is getting what you say you are selling.

8. HR functions: There are paperwork functions in human resources that need to be handled, but as you get larger, someone has to make sure the company mission and values connects with the employees. This has to be tied into the development of your culture and your appraisal processes.

Time and time again, in a single-shareholder business, the owner takes care of all these functional areas except for one or two undesirable things, which are outsourced to a contractor or delegated to an employee. When there are two shareholders, there is more of a balance between them in terms of jobs and wearing hats. But the bottom line is that when you hit a million dollars in revenue, you have to think about these things.

The exception is if you're a web-based business startup and you plan to get a gazillion customers and charge them $9 per month. It isn't easy to keep up with all of that and still make a profit. These kinds of businesses burn through huge amounts of capital before they have a positive cash flow.

THE BLACK HOLE

Between $1 million and $5 million in revenue is what I refer to as the *black hole*. This is the time in your business growth when you're forced to add staffing and infrastructure before you can really afford to. Even if you try to add it as late as possible and maybe even pay for only part-time help, at the end of the day you're going to drive profitability down and risk destroying your business.

Can You Make It Through the Badlands?

In some ways, leading a business through the black hole that lies between $1 million and $5 million in revenue is like leading a wagon train. Let's say I'm in Kansas City, and I buy what I think are enough provisions to get through to California. When I hit the Badlands, I think to myself, "I sure hope I have enough provisions to get through that." If you don't have enough provisions, one of two things is going to happen, and they are both bad. The first is that you are going to die on the trail. The second is you're going to have to turn around and go back and get more provisions, learn some lessons, and try it again.

As you grow from $1 million to $5 million in revenue, you are going to hit some badlands, and you are going to need some resources. The most important resource you will need is extra manpower. It doesn't matter what business you're in. You have to take care of those eight functional areas no matter what size your business is.

At this point, entrepreneurs often get frustrated about their businesses because of their lack of success in hiring staff to perform high-level functions. It usually goes something like this:

> Entrepreneur: *I'm looking to sell my business. (The unspoken reason is because they are in the black hole.)*

Greg: *Okay, great, but what do you think you're going to do next?*

Entrepreneur: *I'm going to find a business where I don't really have to deal with customers or employees. And it will be a business where I really don't have to work a lot, but it makes me a lot of money.*

Greg: *Great. If you find that, then you let us all know about it.*

It would be nice if we could all find a business that makes a lot of profit and comes without employee and customer headaches. But that's not realistic. To get through these challenges, you need to prepare your wagon train and have the right provisions. That means you have to hire people with the right skill sets to make the journey with you, and you have to pay them a market-based wage. If you don't, you're not going to get through the Badlands in one piece.

When you're at a million dollars and you start adding the people you need, you feel really happy about it. You're building a growing business, and you think that anybody you hire will work for you forever. Then you realize at some point, gee, maybe that person isn't the best fit. You have to understand that people are going to change and that one of the keys to success is continually upgrading your staff.

Most Challenging Level of Profitability: $2 Million to $3.5 Million

One of the things I've noticed is that the most challenging level of profitability is between $2 million and $3.5 million. I've also discussed this with one of my clients who does social science research. A social scientist on his staff uncovered the reason. The need to add management infrastructure seems to naturally occur when you have about twenty employees typically, when you're between $2 million and $3.5 million in revenue. Before then, you can get away with not having management structures and moving people from a production role to a management role. But when you have about twenty employees, you have to create a different management structure. This situation typically occurs when you're between $2 million and $3.5 million in revenue.

It's really expensive to hire the wrong people and then replace them. The more times you have to repeat that hiring cycle, the more expensive and more damaging it becomes. The real cost varies, depending on the situation. The usual scenario is that you add labor cost, and the added labor does not increase revenue. Thus, the cost of the additional labor causes an equal drop in net income. Your existing staff see this impact (whether you share numbers or not) and become afraid that they may be let go as the company struggles. Your most capable employees sense this and leave for better opportunities, leaving you with the least productive people. Your lost profit from your hiring mistake leaves you with no excess capital or borrowing capacity to hire a replacement. So you retrench and you assume the role you tried to hire for. You push to stabilize the company so you can make another hiring attempt as soon as you can.

Hire with Care as You Grow

Here's what I always tell people: hire slowly, fire quickly. I'm a big fan of the topgrading concept of hiring when it comes to interviewing and selecting candidates. I strongly encourage my clients to read *Topgrading: How Leading Companies Win by Hiring, Coaching, and Keeping the Best People* by Bradford D. Smart (Portfolio, 2005) to understand the process. I also highly encourage the use of personality profiles as part of the screening process so you understand what makes that person tick. I have tried many different profiles, but I prefer the Caliper Profile from Caliper Human Strategies (www.calipercorp.com).

A lot of growing businesses want to hire someone who has "been there, done that" credentials, but my clients have the least success with this approach. In fact, only about one out of ten has been successful. There are times you must hire experience, for instance, if you need to hire someone to lead your IT department. But usually you need to ask yourself why the "been there, done that" person is available. You'll always get a story to explain it, but do your homework to find the real reason because it's likely you're not getting the full story.

Recently, I was very fortunate to take advantage of a two-day plant tour and program at Dell, the computer manufacturer. I spent a full day with Dell executives, and they said quite a few of their executives were first hired as consultants. This gave the company a chance to get to know them. If Dell decided they wanted to work long-term with a consultant, they hired the person as a full-time executive. This strikes me as a very wise approach for executive-level talent. It gives you time to make sure the consultants don't have just two ideas they continually repeat; better yet, you don't end up paying over and over again for the same two ideas.

Another successful approach is hiring young talent and investing in their education. In fact, at my firm we like to hire people straight out of college. They don't know a lot about anything when they come out of college, but they also do not have any baggage to unlearn. I like having the responsibility to fill their heads full of things I want them to know. A lot of my clients have had their greatest success with young talent who bought into the vision and the dream for the company. These young people are like sponges, and they want to absorb knowledge and information.

You may find the greatest person in the world, but maybe that person isn't right for the role you're hiring for. Too often employers want to attach a bad outcome to a specific person. But actually the employer is probably to blame, because he hired the wrong person for the job. I've found that most of the people who have gone through my business, as well as many others, go on to find great, happy, and successful careers at other places. They just weren't the right fit for my business. The goal is to make sure you don't use a trial-and-error approach to hiring. When you hire someone, you want it to be an informed decision.

Even though we know we have to hire the right people, we still say we want to add those labor costs at the last possible moment. Although you don't want to add the cost of new employees until you have to, you also have to take your time to find the right people and hire them before your business outgrows your ability to manage all the functional areas by yourself.

Your Capital Safety Net

Another important resource you'll need for your journey through the Badlands is capital reserves. You can't get from $1 million to $5 million on borrowed money. How much of a capital reserve do you need to get your company through the Badlands? In other words, what is your capital safety net? It's pretty easy to figure out. Calculate how much cash you need to hire the people you need, then estimate how long it will be before your business can pay the new hires and still remain profitable.

I'm going to challenge you to be specific and model the costs on a monthly basis. You must make assumptions about when the revenue should show up and bring you back to your target profit. It is not as simple as using just the new hire cost, because other costs will rise with the added labor. Forecasting is critical, and I'll cover simple techniques and tools in chapter 10, "Skip the Budget, Learn to Forecast." It is not sufficient to just forecast net income; you also need to forecast cash flows and capital requirements. This will help you know if you have enough resources to get through the Badlands without raising capital or borrowing money.

What if you don't have the capital and you still want to make the journey? In this situation, you might decide to go out and raise capital. Think about getting money from investors, friends, family, venture capitalists, or whomever else you can think of. There's always money in the market. Most venture capitalists will tell you that there isn't a lack of money but there's a lack of good business ideas and good deals. But there's always money for good deals.

I've worked with a number of companies that have raised big money to get through the Badlands. Sometimes they spent the money immediately, either because they needed to or the investor pushed them to spend the money to justify the investment. What happens when people raise the extra money but then end up blowing it? They either go for a second round of financing and give up more of the company, or they find a way to rub two dollar bills together to make a profit. That's how many businesses actually work.

I've had other clients who took the investment money and never tapped into it. They put it on their balance sheet and kept on going. This money was their true capital safety net, which is a great strategy. These clients were committed to being profitable every step of the way from the very beginning of the business. They also had reserves in case they hit unexpected obstacles. That's another key to success.

Successfully Going from $1 Million to $5 Million

During this $1 million to $5 million phase—and this goes back to what you learned in chapter 1—you need to pay yourself a market-based wage and get a return on your investment. Your goal is to still be profitable when you go from $1 million to $5 million, even though you're not going to be as profitable as you were.

You need to reinvest in your business during the $1 million to $5 million phase, but that doesn't mean you shouldn't make a profit during this time. It simply means you leave the profits in your business to fund the growth rather than relying on debt or investors. That's the whole strategy behind paying yourself a market-based wage. You need to live off your wage instead of living off the profits from your business. If you can't do that, just stay in Kansas City. Don't take the wagon train to California. You will not make it through the Badlands.

If you don't have the provisions you need (a capital safety net) and you've already started the hiring process, you might find that you have to downsize to fix your business model and get profitable and healthy again. After that, you can try again to make it through the Badlands and reach California.

$5 MILLION AND BEYOND

Once you get past $5 million in revenue, these same principles apply, just with larger numbers. Hopefully, you have developed a team of people to support you in the process. Entrepreneurs who get past $5 million and continue to survive do so because they have great instincts. Some of my clients have phenomenal instincts, and I think one of the reasons they like working with me is that I help them verbalize what they already instinctively know. They just need someone to observe what they've done and connect the dots.

When it comes to profitability, you have to balance these ideas. But if you don't get the owner compensation right, your profit number will be distorted. That distortion decreases as you approach $20 million or $30 million in revenue. But when owners are at $5 million or less in revenue and play games with their compensation, they're messing up the data that could tell them how healthy their business is. For example, if everything you buy at Sam's Club goes into a business account even though it's groceries, your books don't really mean anything.

Chapter 2 Keys

1. EBITDA is earnings before interest, taxes, depreciation, and amortization. However, as a small-business owner, you should always include interest, depreciation, and amortization as part of your pretax costs.

2. Focus on pretax profit instead of EBITDA.

3. Ignore revenue and focus on gross profit.

4. Your breakeven point is 10 percent:

   5 percent or less of pretax profit means your business is on life support.

   10 percent of pretax profit means you have a good business.

   15 percent or more of pretax profit means you have a great business.

5. As a business grows from $1 million to $5 million in revenue, it will pass through the black hole. To survive, the business owner must have adequate resources to hire additional staff to take responsibility for key functional areas.

6. Learn how to hire the right people, then take time to train them.

7. To get through the black hole, you will need a capital safety net. Prepare a cash flow forecast by month for the time period of the expansion to determine your capital needs.

8. Raise your capital safety net either by reserving profits or by seeking funds from investors.

9. Make a plan to live off your market-based wage and leave every dime of profit in your business as you grow from $1 million to $5 million in revenue.

CHAPTER 3

LABOR PRODUCTIVITY: YOUR KEY TO SURVIVING THE BLACK HOLE

The teams that win are the teams that get the
most productivity for every dollar of labor.

When businesses go through tough times, everybody thinks first about cutting costs. My experience always leads me back to one key factor: labor productivity. Nothing of value happens without labor productivity. Even something like overspending on kitchen supplies can be traced back to a lack of productivity by the person responsible for that task.

When you are below $1 million in revenue, you are a lot closer to what is happening, so you can monitor labor productivity more closely. Once you go past $1 million, your biggest challenge is getting the required productivity for every dollar you spend on labor. I refer to labor dollars instead of full-time equivalent (FTE) employees, because counting heads does not give you the proper understanding of your true profit model. Focus on your gross profit per labor dollar as your key indicator for labor productivity.

First this chapter will give you a close-up view of how two companies navigated their way through the black hole, and you'll gain an understanding of how labor productivity and the black hole are connected. Then we'll take a look at some strategies to manage your profits by controlling labor costs.

SURVIVING THE BLACK HOLE: COMPANY A

In exhibit 3.1, you can see that Company A, in the first year, was slightly under $2 million in revenue (solid line). You also can see that they didn't have a lot of equity built up. Equity is your assets (what you own) minus your liabilities (what you owe). Don't try to make it any more complex than that. Not only that, Company A's pretax profit was close to zero.

Exhibit 3.1: Company A

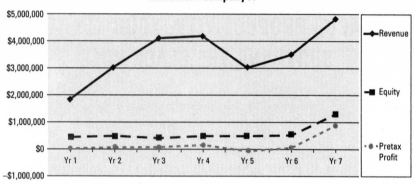

Like most entrepreneurs, they think the solution to the problem of their lack of pretax profit is to grow. They make it all the way up to $4 million in revenue in the next two years. But look at their pretax profit. It didn't go up along with the revenue. See where the revenue flattens out in Years 3 and 4? This is where I started working with the clients. I told them we had to fix their profitability before we could fix their lack of cash and their excess debt.

They made the classic mistake of adding labor to support their growth, but they failed to get enough of an increase in gross profit to drive toward profitability. They had to go back, fix the functional areas that weren't working, and look at the business anew. They had inefficient field labor that was taking too long on simple tasks, people on payroll who were not billable, and sales people who were constantly close to, but never above, the sales goal because they were wasting time by chasing the wrong customers.

Company A set out to improve their profitability so the profit curve would mirror the income curve. In addition, they focused on making the slope of the equity curve equal to the slope of the revenue curve. To accomplish this, they drove the revenue back down to $3 million and then started working their way back up. They examined unprofitable customers and stopped taking on customers that produced low gross profit. Since their revenue declined, it gave them an opportunity to trim the staff and retain the core employees they felt were keepers.

Notice in the graph that their equity went up at the same rate as their pretax profit. Even though their revenue increased, they kept their pretax profit in the business and turned it into equity by reinvesting it in the business. You'll see why that's critical in chapter 4, "Business Physics: The Four Forces of Cash Flow."

SURVIVING THE BLACK HOLE: COMPANY B

Company B took the best approach. Take a look at exhibit 3.2.

Exhibit 3.2: Company B

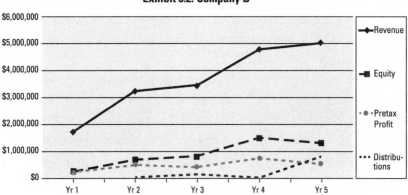

They started off below $2 million in revenue, and they were profitable right out of the gate. You can see that they built equity at a nice pace by being profitable and, unlike Company A, they maintained profitability as their revenue went up. Their pretax profit slowed a little bit, but other than minimal amounts they had to pay in taxes, they kept that profit in the business in the first three years.

Notice that there is a flat year from Year 2 to Year 3. When businesses have early success, they sometimes think they have reached a pinnacle and believe they're as big as they're ever going to get, so they just put their head down and stop thinking about growth. Notice that Company B's pretax profit goes down between Year 2 and Year 3. This is because they hired more people to relieve some of the pressure created by the growth of the business.

The company stayed within the target of 10 percent to 15 percent pretax profit. In Year 2 they were closer to 15 percent, and in Year 3 they dropped back to about 12 percent. This isn't a bad profit, but it's allowing what I call *cost creep*. And a significant component of cost creep is *labor creep*, which is the biggest profit sucker out there. You're doing all those little jobs and you start thinking, "Gee, I really don't like doing that. Let's hire somebody else to do that." We all have details we don't want to take care of. I have four kids and I changed a lot of diapers, but after I got through the first couple, I kind of got over it. Realistically, to have proper labor efficiency you have to make sure that the annoying tasks are distributed to everybody in the company. Labor creep is one of the most common ailments I see. It causes a lot of black hole struggles.

Look at the Distributions line on exhibit 3.2. Notice that Company A doesn't have a distributions line on their graph because they had no distributions. Their profitability is below 5 percent, which is really close to zero. In Company B, the distributions in the first three years reflect only tax distributions because they listened to what I told them. They're building the business, and until they reached their target equity levels, they left that money in the business.

Between Year 4 and Year 5 there is a jump in the distribution level. That's a serious change because I identified that the equity level at the beginning of Year 4 was the base equity they needed to maintain. They didn't need to hold the profits in the company any longer, so they distributed them between Year 4 and Year 5. By the way, the owners of Company B were being paid a market-based wage, so these are *real* profit numbers over and above market-based wages.

See the difference between Company A and Company B? Company A took the typical route of not being profitable before they tried to grow to $5 million. They did not get the necessary productivity of labor to have profit along the way. Company B followed my advice of staying above 10 percent pretax profit at every step along the way and took distributions only to cover taxes until they had nothing drawn on their line of credit and two months of operating expenses in cash. How did Company B remain profitable every year? They did not add labor until the last possible moment, and the owners, along with their management responsibilities, were still productive in the business.

HIRE SMART TO INCREASE PROFITABILITY

As we discussed in the previous chapter, as your business grows, it is important that you hire enough people to take responsibility for functional areas that you can no longer manage. A key talent is to know what tasks to reassign to new hires and what tasks to assign to your current employees.

We have seen that you need to maximize your labor productivity to increase your gross profit, so don't hire an employee for a function that you can do. Depending on the type of business you are in, you might be able to outsource IT, marketing, or accounting, but there are two things that are really hard to outsource: the CEO position and the sales function. I'm not a big fan of outsourcing the CEO function because somebody has to be there every day and be the boss. It's really hard to outsource the sales function because you're stuck relying on an outsider for a very critical component of your business. You won't own the contacts, and that's a really dangerous thing. Unless you have a fear of sales, don't outsource the sales function.

One thing that happens at $5 million in revenue and beyond is that you continue to refine the management team and the people you've brought in to run operations, finance, sales, marketing, and so on. You may find that they hit their ceiling at some point, and you have to continually watch for that. You have to fill all of the business roles as efficiently as you can.

WHAT YOUR BUSINESS HAS IN COMMON WITH THE NFL

As I started studying labor, it dawned on me that every business is like an NFL team. Each team in the NFL operates under a salary cap. For the past sixteen years or so, every NFL team has spent exactly the same amount on labor. This was supposed to create equality among teams, but the New England Patriots won Super Bowls a disproportionate number of times from 2001 to 2009. Most people say that the Patriots' head coach during this time, Bill Belichick, has the ability to get the most productivity in relation to the dollars spent on players' salaries.

A coach has a set amount of money to spend. He can have a great quarterback, but if he doesn't also spend money on a really good left tackle, that quarterback is going to be dead by the third or fourth game of the season. So he has to spend enough money on that left tackle. But wait—now he has to find somebody for his great quarterback to throw to. And he needs a running back to hand the ball to. What about the defense? It has to play well enough to stop the other team. See how interconnected these decisions are?

While looking at some news reports on the Patriots, I found a really interesting example that highlights my point. Back in 2003, the Patriots had Lawyer Milloy, a free safety who was holding out for a new contract. Milloy had a great career with the Patriots. His agent was asking for a contract worth about $4 million, which at the time was the market value of someone with Malloy's skill set. Instead of extending his contract, the Patriots decided to cut him. Milloy's market value wasn't disputed in the marketplace. He got picked up by the Buffalo Bills at that price. That year the Patriots drafted a rookie, Eugene Wilson, and paid him the league minimum: $400,000 for four years. Essentially, the Patriots swapped a known commodity (Milloy, who was a Pro Bowl safety) for a rookie they thought they could develop into an effective player. Wilson didn't start the first game, but he did play during the first game. After that, Wilson started every game for the next four years. The first year that Wilson was the Patriots' free safety, they won the Super Bowl. At the end of Wilson's contract, he was a free agent and the Patriots didn't re-sign him.

The Patriots pride themselves on their ability to maximize output for every dollar they spend on labor. Their success is based on knowing when to hire veteran talent and when to develop new talent. They have been effective at both. I stress the story of developing talent here because most entrepreneurs want quick success and resist training as a viable option for growth.

I know this may sound harsh, but even though you love your employees and you want them to help you win at the game of business, at the end of the day you have a salary cap that you have to live with. Every business has a salary cap. Even an NFL team.

DETERMINING YOUR SALARY CAP

Determining your salary cap is the best way to achieve your required labor productivity. Imagine you've got a million-dollar revenue business. You want the business to have at least a 10 percent pretax profit. If you're not at 10 percent already, you have to try to get there. If you're already above 10 percent, you don't want to go backward.

Take a look at exhibit 3.3 and to see how to start calculating your salary cap.

Exhibit 3.3: Salary Cap: Table 1		
Revenue		$1,000,000
Salaries	(????)	
Nonsalary costs	(????)	
Total expenses		(????)
Pretax profit (10%)		$100,000

At 10 percent, the pretax profit on $1 million in revenue is $100,000. Simple math, right? You can see in exhibit 3.4 that I have $900,000 to allot to two types of expenses: salaries and nonsalary costs.

Exhibit 3.4: Salary Cap: Table 2		
Revenue		$1,000,000
Salaries	(????)	
Nonsalary costs	(????)	
Total expenses		($900,000)
Pretax profit (10%)		$100,000

Your nonsalary costs are easy to come up with. You don't need a consultant to figure it out. The data is in your numbers and you just have to do the math. Ask yourself how much you need for rent, office supplies, telephones, products, and all the other essential things. Costs that stay essentially the same regardless of sales volume are referred to as fixed costs. If you sell goods, your nonsalary costs include the cost of goods sold for the products you sell. You can predict that number because you know what you have to buy. These costs will vary based on sales volume, so they are referred to as variable costs. There are also *step-variable* costs. That means you have to add the cost before you can fully use the cost you are adding.

> Entrepreneur: *Would office space that you rent be an example of a step-variable cost?*
>
> Greg: *Exactly! Your rent is fixed until you outgrow your space and you have to either move or add on. But people are an example of this cost, too. That's why I say that you should add that person at the last possible moment. You don't get full productivity out of a new hire right away, but you get productivity to a point. If I hire a sales manager to manage two salespeople, I get some productivity, but I do not maximize the value of that sales manager until he or she is managing eight to ten salespeople.*

Let's say the number you came up with for nonsalary costs is $400,000. Exhibit 3.5 continues our calculation.

Exhibit 3.5: Salary Cap: Table 3		
Revenue		$1,000,000
Salaries	(????)	
Nonsalary costs	($400,000)	
Total expenses		($900,000)
Pretax profit (10%)		$100,000

Now you can plug in the salaries number, as shown in exhibit 3.6. A little quick math says you have $500,000 to spend on wages. Remember, *your market-based salary is included in that $500,000.*

Exhibit 3.6: Salary Cap: Table 4		
Revenue		$1,000,000
Salaries	($500,000)	
Nonsalary costs	($400,000)	
Total expenses		($900,000)
Pretax profit (10%)		$100,000

It doesn't matter if your employees are part-time, full-time, or if you've hired your cousin or your spouse. You have a $500,000 salary cap. It doesn't matter if you give incentive pay or hourly pay. The sum of all W-2s at the end of the year cannot exceed $500,000. It's no more complex than that.

MANAGING YOUR SALARY CAP

A classic example of someone who ignored the salary cap is a client who did around a million dollars in revenue but just broke even, and he was happy that he didn't owe any taxes. You already know how I feel about that. I said, "You're one bump away from being out of business. You have two choices. You have to cut $100,000 in salaries or you have to not spend a single dime until you produce $100,000 more in gross profit. I don't care which one you pick, but you have to pick one of these two options." A couple of days later, he called and wanted to talk.

> Client: *I have this employee that I've been spending $75,000 a year on. We're trying some new businesses, but we haven't been able to build anything substantial with this employee.*
>
> Greg: *Great! You found $75,000. Now you need to find $25,000 more.*

The client made the adjustment and has been at 10 percent profitability ever since. It is so painfully simple, but everyone wants to make it hard. I guarantee you that if I do those calculations for you, I won't have to tell you who's sucking up the oxygen. You already know.

And you know what? It might even be you. If that's the case, then you need to be realistic. You need to get the most productivity for your labor dollars, and that includes your own salary. As entrepreneurs, we all want our businesses to work. But if you're going to fly in for two days a month and still draw a full salary, you're lying to yourself, so quit taking a salary out of the business. There's nothing wrong with being an investor and just showing up for board meetings with the executive team you hired to run the business.

RAISING YOUR SALARY CAP

Our salary cap example is based on 10 percent pretax profit, but you want to get to 15 percent pretax profit. When you get there, you can do another salary cap calculation like the one in exhibit 3.7.

Exhibit 3.7: Salary Cap: Table 5		
Revenue		$1,000,000
Salaries	($450,000)	
Nonsalary costs	($400,000)	
Total expenses		($850,000)
Pretax profit (15%)		$150,000

This calculation says that your new salary cap, at 15 percent pretax profit, is $450,000. From looking back at exhibit 3.6 we can see that at 10 percent, pretax profit it was $500,000, so now you're over the cap by $50,000. At 15 percent, your pretax profit on $1 million in revenue is $150,000. At 10 percent, it was $100,000. This tells you that 10 percent pretax profit is your bottom line barrier because you need that difference of $50,000 to cover your salaries.

When you get to 15 percent pretax profit, you can add employees to drive your profit back down toward 10 percent, and then you can grow it back to 15 percent again. Your pretax profit and salaries are in flux as your salaries go up and your profit goes down. You can continue this process to get a nice upward-sloping revenue curve like Company B's earlier in the chapter.

If you try to raise your salary cap when you have only 10 percent pretax profit, you'll drive your profit down toward 5 percent, which is the danger area. When I do a salary cap computation for a client, I bracket it with a minimum acceptable target and the maximum target, and I make sure their salary cap runs between those two numbers.

PROFIT VERSUS CASH FLOW: WHY CASH IS A LAGGING INDICATOR

Since managing the salary cap is the key to improving profit, I usually have to reinforce the need for higher profits as an incentive to make the hard decisions on salaries. When I speak to entrepreneurs, I show them three examples of cash flow versus profit: 5 percent, 10 percent, and 15 percent pretax.

Assume the following about each example: This is a service-based business that brings in $1.2 million in revenue a year. By the time they take into account federal income taxes and state taxes, their tax rate is 40 percent. The business spends money on its operating costs for a month and then sends invoices at the end of the month. The next month they do the same. By the middle of the third month, they finally get paid for the first month's invoices. That's the billing cycle in the real world: bill at the end of the month and get paid in forty-five days.

Exhibit 3.8 is the 5 percent pretax profit graph. The solid line represents cumulative profit and the broken line represents cumulative cash flow.

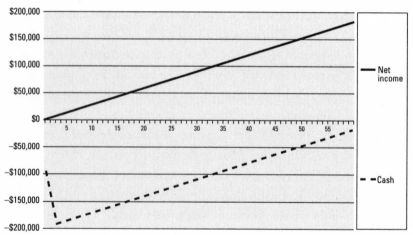

Exhibit 3.8: Cash Flow vs Profit at 5%

This business is immediately $95,000 in the hole in the first month. They go close to $200,000 in the hole before they start earning their way out of it. Notice that it takes over sixty months to break even.

If I change the pretax profit to 10 percent, notice what happens in exhibit 3.8.

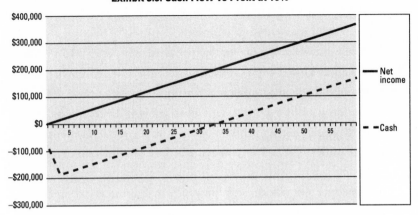

Exhibit 3.9: Cash Flow vs Profit at 10%

The profit line looks great, but the company is still almost $200,000 in the hole. The cash curve is better, and they hit the breakeven point at about thirty-three months instead of at sixty-plus months. All they changed was one thing: they made all their business decisions based on hitting their profit target.

If they make 15 percent pretax profit, look what happens in exhibit 3.10.

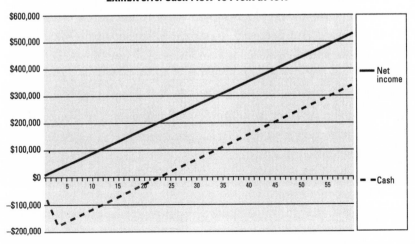

Exhibit 3.10: Cash Flow vs Profit at 15%

Basically, the same thing happens again, but their pretax profits are much higher. They still fall into the same initial hole, but they cross the breakeven point in twenty-one months.

In these examples, you can see that you need to hit at least 10 percent pretax, so that $100,000 pretax profit is definitely the minimum target for a business that is at $1 million in revenue.

This is why profit matters. Everybody is going to dig that cash deficit hole in the beginning. It's just a matter of how fast you can get out of it. There are really only three ways to remedy the cash deficit hole:

1. You can cover it with debt, but you have to use after-tax profits to pay it back.

2. You can cover it with sweat equity instead of getting your market-based wage. But how long can you live with or accept less than a market-based wage?

3. You can get an outside investor, but you have to either repay the investor with after-tax profits or have a good story to persuade the investor that your zero-profit business is worth a lot of money.

This brings to mind a dastardly little thing that happens a lot. You start a company and get a lot of business early because of your credibility and personal charm. Because your customers like you, you may be able to talk them into making a deposit as an advance payment. But that doesn't last very long. Most customers will stretch out their payments as long as possible. Your big-time competition will offer to extend credit to these customers because they can afford to wait for payment. This is one of the barriers to entry that prevent new companies from being competitive.

Chapter 3 Keys

1. Maintain a minimum pretax profit of 10 percent or greater as you grow to the $5 million revenue level, and leave any profits after taxes in the business to fund the growth instead of relying on debt or outside capital.

2. To maximize your productivity of labor, avoid labor creep, and don't hire an employee for a function that you can do. Consider what functions you can outsource, and refine your management team.

3. Calculate and maintain your salary cap (including your own market-based wage).

4. If you are exceeding your salary cap, decide what to do about it. Are you going to hold wages constant until you hit your profit target, are you going to cut staff, or are you going to do some of both?

5. Get to 15 percent pretax profit before you raise your salary cap and drive your profit back down to 10 percent.

6. The higher your pretax profit, the quicker you reach a cash-positive state. Control your profit by getting the most productivity out of every labor dollar you spend.

CHAPTER 4

BUSINESS PHYSICS: THE FOUR FORCES OF CASH FLOW

Cash is the most powerful opportunity magnet ever created.

Typically, entrepreneurs like yourself don't really understand where your profits go. You think, "Hey, I made $100,000, so shouldn't I see $100,000 in the bank?" I can't tell you where every dollar went, but the money's gone because you've either spent it, bought some assets and then sold them, or bought some assets and kept them. Accounting is a closed system. For every debit there's a credit.

When some of this spending is taking place, people don't really think about what they're doing with their money. That's why I like to talk about the four forces of cash flow. Understanding these forces is a major step in preventing what I call *cash cow disease*. Remember, your goal is to keep your cow healthy so you regularly get milk (profits) from it.

THE FOUR FORCES OF CASH FLOW

Unfortunately, the four forces of cash flow are probably in the *opposite* order of what you'd like them to be, but we all have to accept the fact that taxes are the top priority. The four forces of cash flow are as follows, in this order:

1. Paying your taxes
2. Repaying debt
3. Reaching your core capital target (building working capital)
4. Taking profit distributions

Here's a classic example of what happens: You start the year having $100,000 in cash. That's not an insignificant sum, if we're talking about a $1 million (or less) business. Then assume you had a pretax profit of $125,000. That's a good profit number; it's 12.5 percent. So how is it that you have only $25,000 of cash available at the end of the year after paying $50,000 in taxes ($125,000 x 0.40)?

After thinking about it, you realize, Oh, yeah, I did buy a $50,000 SUV for the business. I bought it right at the end of the year to save some money on my taxes. A whole series of "Oh, yeah" moments follow as you realize you made a $50,000 down payment on a condo and you made $50,000 in principal payments on a line of credit. Then you understand that you went from $100,000 in cash to $25,000 because you either spent the money or repaid what you borrowed. Exhibit 4.1 contains the math.

Exhibit 4.1: Where Did the Cash Go? (Step 1)		
Beginning Cash	$100,000	
Pretax Profit	$125,000	
Cash Available		$225,000
Taxes Paid	($50,000)	
Vehicle Purchase	($50,000)	
Distribution—Down Payment on Condo	($50,000)	
Principal Payments	($50,000)	
Total Cash Adjustments		($200,000)
Cash at the End of Year		$25,000

A better approach would have been to start with the $100,000 cash and add your pretax profit of $125,000 for the year (total cash available of $225,000). Then pay your taxes (force #1) of $50,000 and repay the loan (force #2) of $50,000. This leaves you $125,000 before you calculate your core capital target (force #3). This is usually referred to as *working capital*, but after studying it I realized that a better name is *core capital target*. Your core capital target is simply this: two months of operating expenses in cash and nothing drawn on a line of credit. In this example, your company's core capital target is $100,000 (two months of operating expenses). That means you have $25,000 available for distributions (force #4). You know what this means, right? You shouldn't have bought the $50,000 SUV or put $50,000 down on a condo. Exhibit 4.2 contains the corrected math.

Exhibit 4.2: Where Did the Cash Go? (Step 2)		
Beginning Cash	$100,000	
Pretax Profit	$125,000	
Cash Available		$225,000
Taxes Paid (Force #1)	($50,000)	
Principal Payments (Force #2)	($50,000)	
Total Cash Adjustments		($100,000)
Cash Available to Meet Core Capital Target (Force #3)		$125,000
Core Capital Target (2 x $ 50,000)		($100,000)
Cash Available for Distributions (Force #4)		$25,000

Looking at this calculation—and knowing what it means—helps give you the courage to make the right choices. Having the data allows you to quantify it and say you're not going past a specified red line. If you do go past it, you know you're making a really bad choice. In fact, you've stepped into dangerous territory.

HOW THE FORCES WORK TOGETHER

Let's take a look at how all of these forces work together. Then I'll go through each one and explain it in detail. Notice that taking distributions is at the bottom of the list. For clarity, let's define *distributions* as a draw against the equity of the business. Entrepreneurs make these distribution payments in a number of different ways. One of the sloppiest things you can do is try to live off distributions. I've seen clients write checks for groceries, new furniture, home mortgage payments, and their children's education. How serious is this from a tax standpoint? It depends on what type of legal entity you are. If you're an LLC, this isn't so bad because those are just distributions. But if you're an S corporation, this is potentially bad because the IRS will say it really should be salary. Either way, you're taking income out of the business and you don't have a formal methodology in place. You're spending the money but not actually calling it a distribution.

The other problem you run into—and this applies to LLCs, S corporations, and C corporations—is that lawyers will say you're damaging the legal protection of your business. This is called *piercing the corporate veil*, and you're making yourself legally vulnerable as an individual. In almost thirty years of practice, I've dealt with this problem only a few times, but you need to know that piercing the corporate veil is a real issue and can give you legal problems.

I'll talk about this issue more in chapter 5, but for now it's enough to say the best methodology is to manage your personal expenses so you can take care of your business and not live off distributions. Remember, it's about keeping your cow (your business) healthy. It probably won't take as long as you think before you can pay yourself a market-based salary. At my practice we've been able to forecast that date. In many cases businesses are fully capitalized in twelve to eighteen months, and the owners can start paying themselves a market-based wage. Knowing a tentative date will give you the courage to hang on until that day comes.

When it's some unknown date in the future, people are tempted to live off the business prematurely.

There's another reason you don't want to live off your business before it's viable. You want to make sure that you are in a position to cash out of your business.

> Entrepreneur: *I've been told that you should always have your business prepared to sell. Is this true?*
>
> Greg: *Yes. And guess what? If you've worked off the books and done some of these monkey business things, then you're not in any condition to show your financials to a potential buyer.*

A savvy buyer will know if your numbers are lying. Don't compromise your ability to sell your business by making questionable distributions or paying personal bills with company funds.

The Ups and Downs of Operating Cash Flow

In the previous chapter, we looked at graphs of profit versus cash flow for various pretax profit levels. I frequently show my clients the graph in exhibit 4.3 because it shows a true comparison of net income and operating cash flow.

Your operating cash flow starts with your net income for the month; then you add back the difference in the changes in accounts receivable, accounts payable, and inventory (if applicable). You can see that there's a significant disconnect between pretax profit and operating cash flow, and there are big waves in the operating cash flow. This graph looks almost the same in every single business I work with. I'd like to see businesses never go below zero in any one month, but even in my own business, that's not always practical. We have significant heavy times of the year because of tax filing deadlines and some other project deadlines.

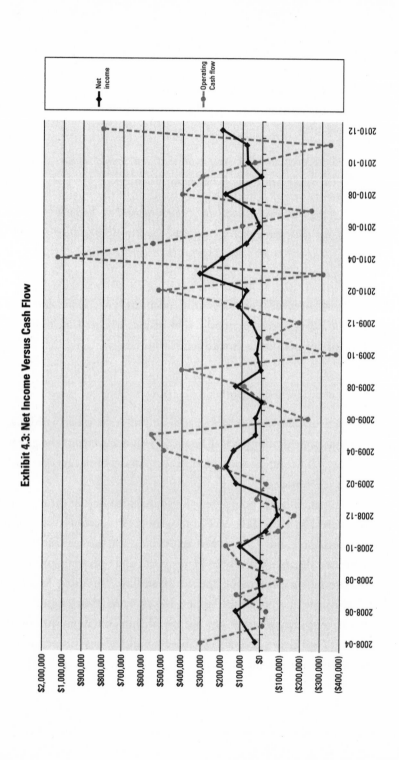

Exhibit 4.3: Net Income Versus Cash Flow

We've been able to make our income more consistent across a twelve-month period because of the monthly business consulting work we do, but for the most part we still have peaks and valleys, as do all businesses.

If you want to be debt free, you need to know how far below zero your operating cash flow is at its worst. In this particular example, the worst downstroke is almost $400,000, so this company's core capital target is $400,000. In almost every case where I monitor this, the worst downstroke is roughly the two months of operating expenses. The way the banking market is today, they can't be certain they'd be able to finance $400,000 if they needed to.

FORCE OF CASH FLOW #1: TAXES

First and foremost, you have to pay your taxes. Every entrepreneur wants to flip taxes to the bottom of the Forces of Cash Flow list. Maybe you had a big month and you want to reward yourself with a trip or a convertible. But before you spend money on anything, you have to set the taxes aside. This is one of the most important things I tell my clients who are on a cash-basis accounting system.

Whenever possible, I recommend cash-basis accounting because there's a much tighter correlation between the cash in your hands and paying taxes on that cash. There are a few rare circumstances when it's better to be on the accrual system, such as a business that gets paid up front for something. But that doesn't happen very often. Even if your customers pay you up front, if your accounts receivable are usually larger than your accounts payable, then you should be on a cash basis. The only time you want to be on an accrual system is if your accounts receivable are consistently lower than your accounts payable. An interesting thing to note about C corporations is they have a requirement to become accrual based at some point. Conversely, S corporations and LLCs can remain on a cash basis no matter how large they get. However, if you have inventory, you are generally required to be on an accrual basis, no matter what type of legal entity you are.

The key with paying taxes is timing. That's where most of my peers in the accounting world fall short. They wait until the year is over and leave you with only bad options. By this time you've bought that convertible, and then you have to round up the money for taxes. You either have to borrow the money or sell some assets for less than what you paid for them. Worse, you have to accept an installment agreement with the IRS, which is not exactly my lender of choice.

In most cases, this is my philosophy: *Don't pay taxes until you absolutely have to without incurring a penalty*. Until you pay the taxes, you have to set the money aside and get it out of your financial calculations so you know it isn't yours to spend.

FORCE OF CASH FLOW #2: DEBT

You can't build wealth until you get out of debt. And make no mistake, getting out of debt really does help you build wealth.

People realized gains during the real estate bubble, but I didn't think the property values made sense. I told my clients to sell the property, get out of debt, and gain a better equity position. Soon after, the real estate market went into a tailspin. Quite a few clients heeded my advice and survived. Others have faced short sales or are hanging on in hopes of a better day. People who take a low- to no-debt approach can handle bad economic news because they live more stable and productive lives. I have clients who are doing quite well—even in the midst of a struggling economy—because they've stuck to this principle.

Types of Debt

There are two types of debt: lines of credit and term debt. For entrepreneurs, credit lines are the equivalent of crack cocaine—it's that addictive. Why? Because when you draw money on a line of credit, you've postponed a hard business decision that should have been made a lot sooner. Sometimes people would rather exhaust their resources than make the hard decisions.

A true line of credit is one that goes to zero for at least thirty consecutive days in a twelve-month period. If you're not doing this, you have what's referred to as an *evergreen loan*. Bank officers look at this and know you're just one bad business cycle away from needing to make an arrangement to pay off your debt.

I don't want you to have anything drawn on your line of credit. If you can be debt free, I'm all for it. But I know there are things you need. For instance, if you need a vehicle for work and you want to buy a Mercedes, I'm not wild about that. But at least it's financed with term debt (a fixed monthly payment over specific period of time) and you can depreciate the cost over the life of the asset (and we consider it part of your market-based wage calculation).

If a new piece of equipment is absolutely essential to the production of the business, I'd rather you pay cash for it. But if you need to buy a piece of production equipment and you know how much productivity and sales you'll get from it, go ahead and finance the equipment with term debt. You will have to remain profitable to retire that debt since you can repay debt only with after-tax profits. If you have to buy a building, that's obviously difficult to buy on a cash basis, but at least it's financed with term debt.

Getting Into and Out of Debt

Sometimes I get a new client whose debt is the result of a classic exchange with an accountant. The client goes to the accountant at the end of the year and has $100,000 of taxable income. The discussion goes like this:

> Client: *I don't want to pay any taxes. What can I do?*

> Accountant: *Well, you can always go buy some equipment.*

But the company didn't go buy equipment for $100,000. They borrowed $100,000 to buy a piece of equipment, which allowed them to take the deduction all in one year. Then, to make matters worse, they took a distribution of $100,000 because they thought they saved that much in taxes. Now they have to devote their future profits to repaying debt instead of having the funds to grow the business.

This approach pushes the client down into a 15 to 20 percent tax bracket—sometimes even lower. I've had clients who went out and bought enough stuff to push them into a zero tax bracket, wasting their personal itemized deductions, which disappeared forever. It's the dumbest tax advice they could get. I want you to pay the least amount of tax allowable under the rules, but I don't want you to distort your rates from one year to the next. You shouldn't be in a 5 percent bracket one year and a 40 percent bracket the next year.

A lot of times I get clients who are already heavily in debt, and they have one of those evergreen credit lines. If you borrow money, you have to forgo any after-tax profits because you have to repay debt with those profits. If you have no taxable profits, you can't repay the debt. When you borrow money, you seal your fate for some period of time in the future. When you take on debt, you're forcing yourself to be profitable in the future or else you'll default. To avoid default, you might end up having to sell the business. Unfortunately, that happens quite often.

FUTURE DEBT

Once I've been successful getting clients out of debt, I talk to them about how to deal with debt going forward. When your debt is either paid off or at least under control, you can think about how to use debt effectively.

You may find yourself in a situation where you exhaust your cash reserves but you are still in need of cash. I have clients in the medical industry whose primary payers are Blue Cross and Medicare. Believe it or not, there are times when the federal government decides not to pay on time. Maybe a budget resolution hasn't passed and there won't be any payment until it passes. But hey, they'll pay you next month or maybe the one after that! Or maybe people are paying you through a contractual arrangement and a contract dispute arises that causes things to seize up. You need to have access to a line of credit because some things are outside of your control, but you know the situation is temporary.

You have to keep your business going during these times. Your cash reserves will cover it to a point, but this situation can become disruptive in a hurry. This is when you should use your line of credit. You're not using a line of credit to fund a losing business. That's what your capital reserves are for, should you choose to use them for that purpose. This is a significant distinction. You should rely on debt only in extraordinary circumstances.

Do not confuse debt with capital. Capital is the cash you leave in the business to fund your receivables and inventory for normal business conditions, and debt is financing for special cases. Once you start financing normal receivables with debt, you are lowering the odds of your business being able to survive a downturn. As you can imagine, clearly making this distinction is a frequent topic in my classes.

> Entrepreneur: *My average account in the disaster restoration business was ninety days overdue. That's one of the reasons I'm not in that business anymore.*

> Greg: *In the disaster restoration business, you often encounter disagreements with insurance adjusters, and then the average turnaround on accounts receivable (A/R) is about ninety days. To survive in that business, you need to use your core capital to handle the slow turnaround on A/R. You'd use your line of credit for what would be considered an unusual disruption in the normal flow of your business.*

An unusual disruption doesn't mean you're not profitable anymore. It's a situation where there's an unexpected delay and you're reasonably sure the cash will show up in the future.

FORCE OF CASH FLOW #3: CORE CAPITAL

The next force of cash flow is reaching your core capital target. Recall from our earlier discussion that your core capital target is two months of operating expenses in cash and nothing drawn on a line of credit. One of my clients develops software, and when the company has good contracts they do well, but when they don't have contracts they have very severe cash-flow problems. Their core capital target is six months of operating expenses. You have to pick the number you're comfortable with.

By default, your core capital target forces you to pay for accounts receivable, inventory, and equipment with capital or term debt. Your target isn't based on equity, because that number might be high for reasons not related to cash. For instance, you might have a high requirement for fixed assets. So keep it simple. You need to be current with paying all your vendors and reasonably current with collecting from all your customers.

Let's go back to our example in exhibit 4.3. This business had an average of $200,000 per month in operating expenses. It is no coincidence that their largest downstrokes in cash flow were approximately $400,000, or two months of operating expenses. There are very few exceptions to this and, unfortunately, very few businesses are above zero for the core capital calculation.

Remember, history is the best predictor of the future. You just need to look back and decide if there's anything you can do to keep that downstroke happening again. There's usually nothing you can do to prevent it, but what you *can* do differently next time is have cash available to cover the downstroke. This way, you can fund that deepest downstroke instead of drawing on your credit line to cover it.

Businesses that have cash and no debt attract magical things. The opportunities that fall into their laps are just amazing. One of my former partners had a client who was in the building supply business. The client was an old-timer who never had any debt and always had over a million dollars in the bank. We were talking to him one day and he said, "I love a recession!" We were stunned. He continued, "I love a recession because I've got cash and I can buy stuff cheaper than anybody because they know that I can pay it. I can work the deals while all my competitors go out of business. I'm the only game in town because I saved my money and they didn't."

This pearl of wisdom is the backbone of entrepreneurism. In 2008, when the credit market seized up and everyone was worried about lines of credit being pulled, I didn't get a single call from a client worrying about that. I got calls from clients who wanted to protect their cash. And that's when I knew that I'd convinced them to live on the cash side of the ledger, instead of the debt side.

FORCE OF CASH FLOW #4: DISTRIBUTIONS

When do you leave money in the business to grow, and when do you take it out? I often answer that with another question: *Do you ever get your money back out?*

Capital formation is the sum of sweat equity, money you invest, and after-tax profits that you keep in the business. When you want to take your money out, there's not a specific number because you don't have an exact amount attached to sweat equity. Capital knows no parent once it comingles with the rest of your business dollars. It's all just capital. Sometimes people think if they put $100,000 in their capital reserve, they'll be able to take that $100,000 back out when the company's running smoothly. That's a fallacy. You still need your core capital target.

Depending on how big your receivables are, how much inventory you have to fund, or how many assets you have to buy, you might be building capital forever. Recall from the black hole stories in chapter 3 that Company B was able to take some distributions of profit because they hit their core capital target (exhibit 3.2). Consistent profits over time allow you to build equity by keeping those profits in the business, which then allows you to hit your core capital target, which then allows you to have excess cash that you can take out without damaging your business's ability to grow or deal with struggles.

This ties back to the basic philosophy that if you pay yourself a market-based wage, then you can live off that salary. Then you can leave the after-tax profits in the business until it is healthy and you reach your core capital target. After that, you can start to take distributions that are beyond the tax expenses.

BUILD A SECURE FOUNDATION

Let's say you've paid your taxes, you have no debt, you've hit your core capital target, and you have $100,000 left over. Before you take that money out as a distribution, ask yourself this question: Is there something you can spend $100,000 on for the business that will get you more than $100,000 back? Don't even consider spending $100,000 just to save 40 cents on the dollar in taxes. That's just a dumb idea.

If the answer is no, then is there something you should build toward that costs *more* than $100,000? Maybe you want to buy a competitor, spin off a new business, or purchase a big piece of equipment that would really change the markets you can get into. Whatever it is, you can keep saving until you hit the number that will help you reach a big goal.

If you're not saving for a big goal, then take the $100,000 distribution and look at your personal life. Do you have any debt or owe any taxes? If not, then what's your liquidity target? Most entrepreneurs who have businesses between $1 million and $5 million need to build up about $2 million of liquid, safe, core assets that give them stability no matter what they're doing in life. When you reach $2 million, you can set your sights even higher. Build a solid foundation first, and then you can enjoy taking some risks.

Chapter 4 Keys

1. Discover where your cash goes (or ask your accountant to help you) by using a format similar to the example at the beginning of the chapter.

2. Set aside your taxes in a separate account on a quarterly basis regardless of when it has to be paid to the tax agencies.

3. Calculate how much cash you need to get your line of credit to zero.

4. Borrow term debt only when you have a clear strategy about how you are going to generate the profits to repay the debt. Understand that you probably won't be able to take distributions while you are repaying the debt.

5. Once you get your business out of debt, do the same for yourself. Yes, that means paying off the house!

6. Build cash by retaining profits until you hit your core capital target. Remember, you can retain only about 60 percent of the profits because you have to pay taxes.

7. Take distributions on a formal basis each quarter only *after* you have covered your taxes and hit your core capital target.

SECTION 2: BUILDING ON THE FOUNDATION

The six chapters in this section build on the concepts you learned in the first section and take your understanding to a deeper level. You will find the "how to" when it comes to tax management and labor productivity.

You'll also learn what type of capital you need for your business and the pros and cons of each source of capital. We'll take a look at the kind of reports you should create and discover the reporting rhythm that makes sense for you. Then you'll learn how to determine what your business is worth from an economic value approach. This will help you manage the process of adding or removing shareholders in your business, regardless if the currency of exchange is money or effort.

Lastly, we discuss the concepts of simplified forecasting to guide your business and discover why forecasting is more effective than budgeting. Most people make forecasting way too complicated, so you'll learn a methodology to create simple rolling forecasts at least every quarter, if not every month.

CHAPTER 5

TAMING THE TAX MONSTER UNDER YOUR BED: TAX MANAGEMENT THAT WORKS

What to pay, when to pay, and how to avoid being a bad example.

In order to pay the amount of taxes you owe the IRS, you have to have a tax management strategy that works. Most people understand that, for the most part, anything that is a business-related expenditure is usually deductible. But this chapter isn't about whether or not you can take a home-office deduction or buy an SUV at the end of the year. You should understand these things, of course, but there are many more tax issues you need to understand so you don't get blindsided.

CHEATERS NEVER PROSPER

I wish it weren't true, but based on my own interactions with people and my discussions with entrepreneurs, I think cheating is more widespread than even the IRS estimates. Since cheating comes in many different forms, the question is whether the cheating is just a little thing or if it translates into big dollars that you should pay to the IRS. If you're doing things that aren't right, you're cheating. But a lot of people try to justify the dubious decisions they make.

One of the ways people soothe their conscience about cheating is by collecting cocktail advice. They think, "Well, I talked to Fred at the party last night and he takes this deduction, and if Fred takes it, then it must be okay." To be clear, I'm not talking about the issues that have an element of grayness to them. For instance, is last night's dinner really a business meal or was it more of a personal nature? I'm talking about things that are *distinct*. Let's take a look at the most common areas of tax fraud. You might be surprised by a few of them.

Paying Yourself a Below-Market Wage

In chapter 1 I explained that using an S corporation to avoid payroll taxes is on the IRS's Dirty Dozen tax scams list, and it's an audit flag. Here's why it's a big issue: Let's say you don't pay yourself a market-based wage of $100,000 so you can avoid paying self-employment, Social Security, and Medicare taxes. That's about $15,000 in tax savings on Social Security and Medicare alone (15.3 percent is the employer and employee portion), which is a significant amount of money. If you have a two-shareholder business, you're avoiding around $30,000 a year in taxes.

People try to excuse this tactic by saying they don't take a salary from the business; they just take distributions. Unfortunately, the IRS doesn't see it this way. They consider distributions to be the equivalent of salaries, especially when you take them in a frequency similar to a paycheck.

Getting Involved in Offshore Activities

Another big area of cheating involves offshore activity. It's certainly a high level of focus at the IRS. There are legitimate offshore activities, of course. In the 2010 health care reform bill, Congress codified the concept of the *economic substance rule*. This essentially says that any transaction conducted merely for the benefit of saving taxes doesn't have economic substance. In such cases, the transaction and the business entity aren't considered legitimate.

There have been some high-profile celebrities who have been caught in offshore activities, and investment firms have been in the news for concealing foreign bank accounts. Don't get involved in offshore activities unless it is essential to the operation of your business. This issue reaches the top levels of the IRS, so it's just not worth it.

Running Personal Expenses Through Your Business

Another area of widespread cheating is the intentional miscoding of expenses, which happens when a business owner fraudulently runs personal expenses through a closely held business. This is different from the sloppy practice of living off distributions that I talked about in chapter 4. I'm referring to when a business owner does something like building a house and paying for it out of the business.

I wish I could say this doesn't happen, but I know it does. Sometimes the expenses aren't as extravagant as building a house, but I know of tax preparers who have found business owners paying for things like home repairs out of their business. This makes me think about the times I've been an expert witness in divorce cases. Spouses have been known to throw each other under the bus for tax noncompliance. It's funny to imagine the IRS sitting through divorce hearings, but that sure would be an easy place to find taxpayers with noncompliance issues.

Working Off the Books

Everybody knows about businesses that take cash and don't report it. But did you know that working off the books also includes bartering? Bartering is not illegal as long as you record it and it is for a legitimate business expense, but it's illegal to trade a legitimate business expense for something that is for your personal benefit.

There have been a lot of exchanges set up across the country where people try to barter legitimately, but arrangements like this usually struggle. If the business you're bartering with goes out of business, you're left holding the bag with unused credits. Bartering may seem simple, but it's actually more complicated than using cash. Humans began using currency thousands of years ago to simplify business transactions and avoid the problems with bartering. Somebody always gets the short end of the deal. That is why I advise my clients to avoid bartering and stick to cash payments.

Bartering can also be fraudulent. Let's say I have a tax preparation business and a hair stylist needs my services. The stylist agrees to cut my hair in exchange for a free tax return. This is wrong because I can't deduct haircuts as a business expense. But believe me, people have tried it!

Not Filing Tax Forms for Subcontractors

If you have a subcontractor, you must give that person a 1099. You're not helping a subcontractor by not issuing a 1099. At my firm, we require subcontractors to fill out a W-9 form and give their taxpayer ID number before they can get paid. That way we don't have to chase them down at the end of the year when we send 1099s. You're only hurting yourself if you aren't vigilant about this, since you are aiding them in avoiding taxes. The government can only collect from the people who are compliant, so if I am compliant, why would I want to help someone cheat? In the end, it makes me pay a larger share of the taxes.

This rule is not as bad as a lot of people think. I've found that the people who complain about the 1099 filing requirements are the people who really don't want to report their income.

CASH VERSUS ACCRUAL

So you did your taxes and you didn't make any money. The most common reason for this is that you used cash-basis reporting. Simply put, if you work this year and bill the client $100,000 for your services, but at the end of the year the client hasn't paid you, then you don't have to report the income this year. You don't report it until you get paid. But the thing is, you haven't made any money yet. You can't feed your family based on $100,000 in receivables.

The cash-basis method is a very valuable approach. It's the best methodology to reflect when the cash shows up as well as when it doesn't. The only time you wouldn't want to use a cash basis is when you consistently get paid before you have to pay your vendors, which is rare.

In the previous chapter I briefly mentioned the rare circumstances when you might need to use an accrual system. To understand these differences, you have to look at the balance of your accounts receivable less your accounts payable and accrued expenses. If your accounts receivable are $250,000 and your accounts payable plus accrued expenses are $100,000, you have $150,000 of taxable income that you are postponing to a future year. This is because you have not collected the accounts receivable yet, and you have not paid the accounts payable or accrued expenses.

If you get paid in advance for services, it's still taxed whether it's cash or accrual, unless it is contractually structured as a refundable deposit. It may still be hard to win the argument in an audit if all of the facts are not in your favor. If you decide the risk is not worth it, use the accrual basis and accrue the expenses when they correspond to the revenue.

ARE YOU THIS ENTREPRENEUR?

I've already mentioned how spending money to avoid taxes is a dumb idea. This example further demonstrates how this hurts both you and your business. Let's assume Rick is my top sales guy. I owe Rick a $100,000 bonus at the end of the year because he knocked it out of the park with sales. At the end of the year I say, "Rick, good job! I owe you $100,000, but unfortunately the IRS is going to take 40 percent of that in payroll taxes, income taxes, and state taxes. I know how much you despise the IRS because you've got those bumper stickers on your car that say so. I decided to stick it to the IRS on your behalf!" So I take that $100,000 I was supposed to pay Rick and spend it on new computers for the office. How do you think that makes Rick feel?

As the owner of a business who's getting rid of $100,000 of profit so you don't have to pay any taxes, you're just like Rick, the sales guy who didn't get his bonus. You wasted $60,000 of the after-tax money that you needed to build wealth and repay debt so you could avoid paying $40,000 in taxes. I've seen this year after year and client after client. You're just lying to yourself when you take this approach.

TIMING IS EVERYTHING

That leads us into the biggest issue: the timing of taxes. Let's take a closer look. Say you have $100,000 in profits, but you decided not to take the money out of the business in distributions. You want to avoid paying taxes, so you buy a piece of equipment with 100 percent financing. You'll lower your tax bracket and pay as little as possible this year, but next year you'll pay at the top bracket. If you had waited to buy the equipment, you could have paid an average of 25 to 28 percent per year. You have to think about taxes on an ongoing basis.

Most entrepreneurs either don't want to know what their taxes are or they don't have a tax advisor who constantly monitors what the tax impact of business decisions will be. You have a tendency to pay taxes on business profits when you file your tax return, which is usually somewhere between April and October of the following year. If your pretax profits are up one year and down the next, you'll underpay your taxes in the good year, and you'll pay a lot of taxes for the prior year during your bad year. This kind of cycle is a business killer. Realistically, you should be paying last year's taxes with the tax funds you set aside last year. Even if that year is a bad year, those tax payments are being made with cash that was already set aside for the purpose, so it's okay.

Now you can see why tax management is the first of the four forces of cash flow that we discussed in chapter 4. Almost every entrepreneur who has a flow-through entity—which is an S corporation, LLC, or partnership—is confused about whether the company's taxes are coming from this year's profits or from last year's profits.

A lot of people invest in LLCs and S corporations and complain that they pay taxes and never get any money out of their business. If the tax payments are timed correctly, that shouldn't happen. People think taxes are complex. At a detail level, they are, but at a macro level, they aren't. All you're trying to do on a quarter-by-quarter basis is get close enough to the actual amount you'll owe so you know whether to send a payment or hold it back. Either way, you have to take the money out of your financial equation.

Have your tax advisor create a simple tax calculation template that you can review each quarter, or you can download a tax calculation spreadsheet for an LLC or an S corporation from my website, www.seeingbeyondnumbers.com. The one we use is for a cash-basis business, so you can measure where you currently stand. It does quick calculations so you can get an idea of what your tax reserves should be.

TWO APPROACHES TO TAX TIMING

In the last chapter we talked about how waiting until the end of the year to think about your taxes leaves you with only bad options. In this section I will describe two approaches to timing your tax payments to avoid those bad options. But first let's look at underpayment penalties. The IRS put the underpayment penalty in place to make you pay your taxes evenly throughout the year and not wait until the end of the year—unless you meet the exceptions for the prior year taxes paid or the pay-as-you-go approach, which I'll describe shortly.

Safe Harbor

The first approach to timing tax payments is called *safe harbor*. This year you pay either what you paid in taxes last year, or, if your *taxable income* (gross income from all sources less deductions and personal exemptions) is above a certain threshold, you pay 110 percent of what you paid last year (see www.irs.gov and search for Form 2210 instructions for the current rules). In the latter case, if you paid $10,000 in taxes last year, then you should plan to pay $11,000 this year ($10,000 x 1.10). If your pretax profits go way up and you owe $1 million in taxes by April 15 of next year, you won't owe the difference until April 15, and you will not incur an underpayment penalty.

You can see the difference in scale of going from $10,000 in taxes one year to $1 million in taxes the next year. It's obviously important that you have the million dollars when it comes time to pay your taxes, but you'd be surprised at how many people don't plan for this. I've had clients who had to sell their business, or at least segments of their business, to pay taxes. If my clients have a special income event and the IRS rules allow them to wait until April 15 to pay taxes on that, I tell them to buy a Certificate of Deposit that matures on April 10. This prevents them from touching that money for any reason.

Pay as You Go

The second approach is to pay as you go and make estimated payments on your taxes throughout the year. The payment dates are divided into four periods:

January 1—March 31	Due April 15
April 1—May 31	Due June 15
June 1—August 31	Due September 15
September 1—December 31	Due January 15 of next year

To use this method, ask yourself what you made in the first quarter, and calculate the tax on that (40 percent). If you pay that amount, you don't incur an underpayment penalty. For the second quarter, take your profit to date times the tax rate minus what you paid as an estimate in the first quarter. That's what you owe for the second quarter. Repeat this for the third and fourth quarters.

This is the easiest way to track what you owe. The only danger of the pay-as-you-go approach is that you can have really good first and second quarters but then have some losses in the third and fourth quarters. This results in your annual income being exaggerated in the first half of the year, so your tax payments for that time period may be larger than needed, and you will have to file your return before you can get your overpayment back. When I manage this for my clients, I have them pay the *least* amount possible under the safe harbor or the pay-as-you-go methods. I have them create a separate bank account to hold the tax money for any taxes they owe above the safe harbor method.

Timing Tax Payments to Your Best Advantage

If my clients' taxes for the previous year were higher because their taxable income this year is down, I have them use the pay-as-you-go method. I don't want them burning up good core capital by paying their taxes way too far in advance, which is what would happen if they used the safe harbor approach. Their core capital is a very precious resource, so it's not good enough for me to just make a simple calculation and tell them to base their payments on 110 percent of the prior year tax if they exceed the threshold.

TAXES AND THE PERSONAL SIDE OF YOUR FINANCIAL LIFE

Let's look at our favorite cow analogy and extend it to your personal life. If you don't keep your cow healthy so you can milk it every day, you're not going to have an economic engine to be able to distribute wealth to the personal side of your life. Many times people try to live off the profit distributions of the business, and then there's nothing left over for wealth creation. Here's where the tax side of that makes a big difference.

A Perfect Scenario

In a perfect scenario, you should pay yourself a market-based wage for what you do. Then withhold taxes from that wage as if the business is going to make zero profits. The goal is to be able to take your salary, pay your taxes on your salary, and live off the net amount. Base your lifestyle on the net amount, and you won't have to rely on distributions to pay your personal bills.

If you make $100,000 a year in wages for your role in your business, put that salary plus your spouse's salary into a tax projection and determine what your withholdings should be to break even—not to get a refund, but to break even. To determine how much should be withheld from your salary, assume that the business will make nothing. If the business makes a profit beyond your salary, the business should make a *tax distribution* to cover the taxes it caused you to pay.

There's no terminology within the tax code that refers to a distribution as a *tax distribution* or a *profit distribution*. I use these terms to differentiate the purposes of distributions. They can be made to cover taxes, or they can be made to distribute profit. When your business makes a profit on a quarter-by-quarter basis, the first distributions are made to pay the taxes. It is imperative that you don't spend this on anything else. Either make an estimated tax payment or set it aside to pay taxes later.

Business owners commonly misunderstand that your taxable income in an S corporation or an LLC is not based on your distributions (except in rare circumstances); it is based on your share of the net profit of the business, regardless of whether you take distributions or not. In some multiple-shareholder cases, one shareholder has to pay taxes though another one doesn't. When tax distributions are paid to shareholders, one or more of them will invariably spend it instead of paying taxes with it. Then at tax time they will come back to the business and ask for cash flow help.

After the tax distributions have been made, you can take profit distributions. Use them to build your emergency fund and repay your personal debt until it's gone. After that, you can start investing and building true wealth.

A Nightmare Scenario

A nightmare scenario is when you're living off your salary *and* your distributions. You haven't set aside anything for taxes. Your tax preparer extends your tax return until October, which is the extended due date, and you find out on the due date that you owe taxes for the profits the company made last year as well as your salary.

Because you don't have money set aside for taxes, you use the IRS as your creditor and do an installment agreement. Or you might start thinking that next year will be better, so you just don't file your return. You figure the IRS won't know about it, and you'll get caught up financially so you can pay the taxes. One year turns into two, which turns into three, then five, then six. I've had people come to me who have essentially gone underground for five to seven years, and they say they're ready to become legitimate and get caught up. It's so sad when businesses haven't filed their tax returns. Eventually, something will trip the wire with the IRS and they'll find out you've been underground.

Don't take that chance with your business. Choose the perfect scenario and avoid a nightmare for yourself and your business.

Chapter 5 Keys

1. Don't justify cheating with cocktail party advice, and watch out for areas of tax fraud.

2. Understand if you should use a cash-basis system or an accrual-basis system in your business.

3. Spending a dollar to save 40 cents in taxes is not a wise choice!

4. Calculate your tax liability each quarter whether you are required to pay it in or not.

5. Know whether you should use the safe harbor or pay-as-you-go approach to making tax payments. Be aware that the right approach for you could change each year.

6. Set your market-based wage, have your taxes taken out of that wage, and take care of your lifestyle using your net pay. Leave your distributions in the business to first cover business taxes and then build wealth.

CHAPTER 6

HOW TO MAXIMIZE YOUR LABOR PRODUCTIVITY

*Opportunity is missed by most people because it is
dressed in overalls and looks like work.*

—Thomas Edison

Welcome to what I refer to as the *salary economy*. I call it this because the market affects the way you manage your salary cap whether you want it to or not. Understanding these market forces helps you effectively manage the salaries in your business. Some people believe they can take a minimalist approach and pay people the least amount possible. In this chapter, you'll learn that there's a middle ground between paying too much and paying too little. It's important to understand these concepts because your gross profit per labor dollar is the second most important key performance indicator for your business (remember that the size of the check you wrote to the IRS is number one).

PRODUCTIVITY FROM EVERY DOLLAR OF LABOR SPENT

In chapter 3 I said the number one thing that causes you to be either profitable or unprofitable is how much productivity you get out of every dollar you spend on labor, including your own market-based wage. I'll use my company as an example. I have to get $1.80 of gross profit (revenue less direct out-of-pocket costs for subcontractors or travel, not including any in-house labor) for every $1.00 I spend on labor to reach my profitability target, regardless of whether that $1.00 is paid to an administrative person or a production person. You might think administrative people don't generate gross profit, but they do! They take care of tasks that allow billable people to be more billable.

In every business, each dollar spent on labor has to show a demonstrable output for gross profit. Here's a simple metric to keep in mind: If you aren't at 10 percent pretax profit, use what you learned about managing and raising your salary cap in chapter 3 to determine how much labor you need to cut or how much gross profit you need to add to get to that number, and then try not to add staff until you get to 15 percent pretax profit. This is how you control internal growth and profitability.

What people often do is add five people at once. You typically can't absorb that cost. It's like taking five daily vitamins in a single day. Your body can't absorb it. It's more efficient to hire people on a more regular cycle and give them more direct attention.

CAN CULTURE AND PROFITABILITY COEXIST?

Every business has a culture, and it's an important part of the foundation of your business. Your challenge is to find a way for your culture and profitability to play nice with each other. I have seen it succeed in my company and in my clients' companies. I have also seen companies fail when they overemphasized one over the other. It's a good idea to document your culture and how it ties into your profitability as a business because the more you document it, the easier it is to live it and maintain it.

You can take a look at my firm's culture document on our website, www.seeingbeyondnumbers.com. You can use it as a template and adjust the wording to fit your needs. It basically states what our plans are, who we are, why we believe certain things, and how we hold people accountable. My COO sends an e-mail at the beginning of the week that highlights one segment of our culture document to let everyone know what our focus of the week is.

One of the advantages of having a culture document is to avoid the "emperor has no clothes" scenario that every entrepreneur faces. One way I avoid this is by encouraging a long-term employee to be brutally honest with me. I tell her to let me know if I'm ever just out in left field and not really paying attention to what is going on. If there's someone in the business who can be a knowledgeable sounding board and has a high comfort level with you, encourage that person to come to you and tell you the hard things. This has to be someone who will say, "That sounds great, but that's not going to happen because here's how you're coming across to everybody else."

Owners commonly want to have a family atmosphere. This is admirable, but understand that a company with a great culture and no profits is going to die. You have to make sure your culture doesn't excuse people from getting their jobs done. There's an economic relationship between productivity and the amount you're paying people to get things done. If this relationship isn't balanced, you have a flawed business model.

THE SALARY ECONOMY

This is where the salary economy comes in. Essentially, your goal is to avoid overpaying or underpaying your employees. Both situations are bad, but the entrepreneurs who underpay employees tend to have companies that struggle in the long run due to high employee turnover. Companies in the same industry that pay higher wages and have fewer employees might be more profitable than companies that pay lower wages and have more employees, but it's a very delicate balance. You can't assume that if you pay higher wages you'll get more productivity, and you can't assume that if you pay lower wages you'll get the same productivity.

Never give an employee a cost-of-living adjustment. If you do, you will have many employees asking for a salary increase based on what they need to make a living. The amount they choose to spend in their lives is not your problem. What you pay them should be within a market-based range for their roles. My approach to this frequently raises questions in the entrepreneur classes I teach. Participants want to know if I look at cost-of-living adjustments differently if a period of severe, long inflation affects my own business. What they really want to know is whether the cost of living drives the salary economy or if the salary economy drives the cost of living. I believe the salary economy drives the cost of living. Salary is like a gas; it expands into the chamber of life and you consume it, for the most part, so you adapt based on whatever salary is available to you.

HOW MARKET FORCES IMPACT SALARIES

I have a lot of clients who overpay people. This is often a classic example of having an employee who claims to have fifteen years of experience but actually only has *one year of experience fifteen times*. This kind of employee is worth no more than an employee who has one year of experience, so years of experience often don't count for much. The important thing is what people know and if they have the capacity to produce. Some people think it's great to be with a company twenty years, but there are plenty of people who've worked in the same job for twenty years and just showed up for work and did the same thing every day. In this case, a fresh person with no experience can easily do that job.

Eventually, market forces flush out both sides of the equation. Let's say you have a person who's outperforming a higher-paid employee. You have two choices. If the higher-paid employee represents the true market value, you have to raise the lower-paid employee to that salary level. If the higher-paid employee isn't worth the money, you have to either transition that employee out of the business or find a way to improve that employee's performance. In rare cases, I have lowered the pay of the underperformer, but that is usually a short-term fix until that person chooses to leave.

Employees often end up being underpaid because they came into the company at entry-level positions. Even though you inch their pay up every year, you suddenly realize you're adding new people who are making the same amount as employees who came into the business two years earlier. Now you have employees who have been there for two years and are making an entry-level wage. You must decide if those people are underpaid and worthy of a higher salary.

During the five years from 2005 to 2010, I saw both ends of the spectrum in terms of available employment. When the unemployment rate was below 5 percent, employers had to overpay to attract desirable employees. However, since 2008 a lot of experienced people have become increasingly desperate. Someone who's used to making $75,000 to $100,000 might be willing to accept $40,000 to $60,000 just to get a foot in the door. In a downturn, certain industries collapse, and they aren't going to come back anytime soon. The people from those industries will take serious wage cuts because they have to start at the beginning and learn a new industry. Be careful about hiring people for $40,000 a year when they're used to making $80,000 a year. You need to have a career path that gets them back up to $80,000, because when their original industry bounces back, they'll leave you to get their $80,000 job back. You often have to consider these transitional people to be short-term employees.

USING SALARY SURVEYS

So how do you make sure you pick the wage that's in line with the market? In chapter 1 I talked about using salary surveys to determine market-based wages, but remember that they can be inflated. You can also gauge market value by talking to your peers in the same industry and looking at local wage surveys. My local chamber of commerce publishes an excellent wage survey each year. We participate and have access to the survey. It's been a very valuable source of information. Association wage surveys are probably valid only for your employees because, as we've discussed, owners play games with their salaries and distributions.

Despite their shortcomings, salary surveys can help you define salary ranges. My firm has administrative positions, entry-level accounting positions, client manager positions, and specialist positions. Salary ranges are established for each position, and they take into account the required skill sets and education. For production positions, we look at the productivity needed based on the revenue and gross profit requirements. Not every business can tie profitability or gross profit or revenue on a per-employee basis, but many can. If you have that ability and there's software that allows you to capture the data, it's one of the best ways to understand and evaluate employees.

Be aware that when you have this kind of data, you can end up with a moral dilemma. Let's say you have an employee who is producing significantly more than another employee, but they have similar salaries. You have to honestly look at the data and decide if you're going to pay the more productive person a higher salary or pay the other person less.

EVALUATION PROCESS IS KEY

Your employees need to understand what is expected of them in terms of productivity, and the best way to accomplish this is through the employee review process. Although you need to deal with issues as they come up, you need to have a formal meeting with each employee at least twice a year.

I focus on career planning and career path in employee reviews. Realistically, my goal is to invest in my employees' careers for as long as they want to be at my firm. We discuss their career goals and answer a few questions. Do they require additional education? Do they need different skill sets to get promoted to a higher level? The more closely you define and help develop an individual's career, the more likely you are going to have a long-term employee. Even if an employee's desire goes beyond working at my company, it's still in my best interest to help the employee develop so that person can have a successful career. As long as the employee works for me and I'm getting productivity for the money I'm paying in salaries, that's a good thing. I want my employees to understand that they are welcome to work in my company as long as we are both getting a fair exchange.

It's my responsibility as the CEO of the company to provide my employees with a vibrant environment, a fair wage, and a good culture. When there's a point where it doesn't work anymore, I'll help an employee transition into a new job. For the most part, I've taken a hard view that says we're all replaceable—including me! But if we try to help each other become the best we can be, it leads to a much better cultural experience for everybody. You'll even find that some people stay far longer than they otherwise would have.

Identify the Top Three to Five Skill Sets for Each Role

A lot of business owners get too detailed when they evaluate what matters in each job. Focus on the top three to five skill sets that are required to maximize productivity for each job. You can easily list twenty to thirty skill sets that you really want a person to have, but in terms of evaluating whether those skill sets match that person's compensation and productivity, it's going to come down to three to five that matter the most. For your sales department, you might list effective use of Salesforce.com, proposal drafting, and lead generation. For your receptionist, you might list phone etiquette, document management, and proposal editing and production. As you do your performance reviews with these skill sets in mind, you will be able to give more specific direction on how employees can improve their performance and how you can help them achieve their productivity potential.

At my firm, we identified five skill sets for our technical people. The first three are being able to project and prepare personal tax returns, project and prepare business tax returns, and set up and run a set of books. A lot of accountants believe bookkeeping is beneath them, but many times when I'm discussing problems with clients I need to tell them how to fix something in QuickBooks. The fourth skill set is the ability to prepare a reviewed financial statement, which looks exactly like an audit, but the opinion letter is different and the underlying work is different. The fifth skill set is the ability to create an integrated balance sheet, profit and loss and cash flow forecast from a blank Excel spreadsheet. We take historical data from our clients and create a forecast called a *momentum forecast* that is based on the movement of real data rather than input from the client.

Employee Evaluations That Will Drive Culture and Profitability

Now that you have identified the required core skill sets, let's discuss the five critical areas I use to evaluate each employee. These areas are in order of importance to us and allow us to keep true to our culture and drive profitability.

Key #1: How Good a Teammate Is the Employee?

Our front-desk person is the quarterback of the office. Just about every business has someone like that. Her customers are both external customers who walk in the door and every other person she supports inside the business. If she is cold toward either external customers or her fellow teammates, it doesn't matter how good her skill sets are. Every employee (and the owner!) has to be a good teammate to fit into our culture and represent the firm well.

Key #2: How Well Does the Employee Connect with External Customers?

There are a lot of people who are technically sound but don't do well with people. Maybe you think you can hide these people in a corner and hope they don't have to talk to customers, but at some point they'll likely have contact with a customer. Do you want those people to represent your business?

Key #3: How Productive Is the Employee?

I have found that there are two types of workers: tortoises and hares. Tortoises stay at their desks. They stay focused and they work, work,

work. They may not necessarily be fast, but they stay at it. Hares can whip out tasks, but they spend the next hour telling *everyone* how fast they got it done. The problem is they can't maintain that pace; they get burned out and need a lot of time to recharge. So be careful in terms of evaluating productivity over short periods of time versus longer periods of time.

Watch for employees who have to expend a large number of hours to be productive. There are times when you need people to put in extra hours, but it should be because you need the additional productivity. You don't need people to work extra hours if they were unproductive for a couple of hours that day. Beware of employees who come in an hour late and then stay late to make up time or employees who take extra breaks and extra time at lunch to surf the Web or make personal phone calls. You can use timesheets to find out people's true productivity. Timesheets don't lie, but sometimes it's very painful to recognize what's going on.

Key #4: Does the Employee Contribute at Your Targeted Profitability Levels?

Clearly you have to make a profit from every employee or else you have a broken business model, so you have to evaluate each employee in terms of profitability. Even if you don't have a gross profit component to compare against an employee's performance, you can still look at profitability. If you have a person who's making $50,000 a year, look at the things that person does. If you can hire somebody for $35,000 a year to do the same thing, then you're losing $15,000 a year.

It's not uncommon for someone who's doing a $35,000-a-year job to creep up to $50,000 a year. This is especially true when a job initially required technical experience, but maybe the technology is more common now and anyone can be taught those skills. That's a tough one in terms of salary cap management, but it gives you a basis of communication with that employee, which leads you back to career development.

Key #5: Core Competencies: Have the Employee's Responsibilities and Skills Increased?

When people have stepped up and taken their performance to another pay level, I adjust their salaries as soon as I can. I spent three years as a controller for a bank, and in that period there were three specific times when my roles and responsibilities changed. Each time the CEO of the bank gave me a pay adjustment. I try to follow this example and not wait for a review cycle to adjust someone's pay.

I tell my staff that their pay changes for only one of two reasons: if the salary economy changed and we adjusted the pay scale or if they moved up a level. When the latter happens, I say something like, "You've moved from level two to level three to become a client manager." The employee knows that the pay scale moves up by a certain amount. I make it clear what the person will do differently as a level-three client manager, and I explain what the employee needs to improve on to get to level four. By doing this, I can give people definitive guidance and provide a focus to their career paths.

IS OPEN-BOOK MANAGEMENT RIGHT FOR YOU?

Jack Stack, president and CEO of SRC Holdings Corporation (formerly Springfield ReManufacturing Corp.), has written extensively about the concept of open-book management (OBM). His ideas are summarized in his book *The Great Game of Business* (Doubleday/Currency, 1992). OBM basically allows everyone in the company to see and talk about the company's financial information.

My firm practices a version of OBM in which we share *all* the information. Everyone knows what everyone else makes. My staff know what I make, they know what the firm's numbers are, and they have access to the firm's financial data. I want them to understand the part they play in our success. I'd rather deal with facts than rumors. I can explain any financial decision I make, but if I'm inconsistent with any decision, I'm held accountable for it. The challenge is that some employees are a little uncomfortable with this approach. My response is that they'll become more comfortable as they start to understand that they're being paid a fair wage for what they produce. That's an essential part of our culture.

When employees ask why someone else is making more than they are, it's an opportunity to talk with them about how they can make more money. I show them what their productivity needs to be to get to the next salary level. I'm not running a charity—my business runs under the same laws of business physics as everyone else's—but I have to be able to talk through the perceived inequities.

Some business owners are concerned about sharing numbers because when employees leave for a different job, they might share the numbers with a competitor. My viewpoint is that my numbers don't really matter. It's more important to me that my fellow practitioners do the things we do so they can help more clients run profitable businesses. The market is huge; the number of competitors isn't one of my challenges. My biggest challenge is how quickly I can grow college students into client managers so I can expand my business.

Many business owners practice OBM with the exception of sharing salary information. I struggle with that approach because, as I said at the beginning of the chapter, your gross profit per labor dollar is the second most important key performance indicator for your business. If you and your management team are not comfortable explaining the numbers, I would not recommend using OBM. However, if you can become confident in explaining your data to your team, I think you will find OBM very liberating.

BE CAREFUL WITH INCENTIVE PLANS

Contrary to popular opinion, throwing money at a problem doesn't change the outcome. Most entrepreneurs look to incentive plans as a substitute for management and leadership. I urge my clients to not make this mistake and encourage them to evaluate their management and leadership skills and make improvements where needed before any incentive plan is implemented.

I've played with incentive plans, and very few of them created the desired outcomes. Before I devise an incentive plan for an employee, I want to see a personality profile to find out if the person is motivated by money and driven by incentive plans. Very few people are motivated this way. People will tell you that getting more money will change their performance, but it's usually more effective to use small amounts of money along the way to recognize outstanding achievement.

Executive Incentive Plans

As you get larger, you may have to implement an executive incentive plan to stay competitive with your market. You can go to my company's website, www.seeingbeyondnumbers.com, and see an example of a plan for executive team members where we tie in two components. The first component is a gross profit dollar scale that shows what executives can earn and what the business performance needs to be in terms of gross profit. This has various levels: a minimal acceptable performance, a target performance, and a stretch performance. In some cases, there can even be a level beyond stretch performance.

The second component is the labor efficiency ratio I mentioned earlier, which may range from $1.80 to $2.20 of gross profit for every $1.00 the company spends on labor. If a company hits its gross profit dollar performance level and the labor efficiency ratio, profitability is almost assured to hit the bottom line. But if the company hits only the gross profit performance and overspends on labor to make it, the profit target is not reached, and the executive bonus is reduced or even eliminated.

Forecast Your Incentive Payments

I use a miniature business forecast for each component of my incentive plan models. If the business hits a certain level of gross profit performance and a certain level of labor efficiency, I know what the pretax profit will be before incentives. I can also see what the total incentives will be so I'll know what percentage of profitability will be going to an employee.

So many times people just pick numbers out of the air and say, "I'll give you 1 percent of revenue or 10 percent of profit." They don't go through the mathematical implications of what they are giving away. In many cases, every dime of additional growth benefits an employee who may not have caused it. You're the one who's taking the risk of running the business, so unless you forecast incentive payments, you could be throwing good money after bad. Pick whatever number makes sense after you forecast it and understand the financial implications.

Payout Plans

The other part of an incentive plan is how you pay it out. In Jack Stack's *The Great Game of Business* he describes a 10, 20, 30, 40 percent methodology he used to avoid overpaying incentives early in the year:

1. In the first quarter, calculate the annual bonus by annualizing the first quarter's productivity. The employee would be paid 10 percent of the annualized bonus.

2. In the second quarter, take six months of performance, annualize it, and then calculate 30 percent of the annual bonus. Subtract the 10 percent you paid in the first quarter, and pay the employee the other 20 percent. At this point, the employee has been paid a total of 30 percent.

3. In the third quarter, take nine months of performance, annualize it, and then calculate 60 percent of the annual bonus. Subtract what was paid already in the first and second quarter, and then pay out the balance. It's self-correcting each quarter. The employee is always getting what's due today minus what's previously paid.

4. In the fourth quarter, the bonus is 100 percent of the annual bonus less what has been previously paid in the first three quarters. By leaving the largest payout until the end of the year, some businesses can still make up for poor performance earlier in the year with a Hail Mary approach.

This kind of incentive plan is based on annual performance, but some businesses base incentives on quarterly or monthly performance, especially when they have a poor history of putting four solid quarters of performance together. The problem with these plans is that they encourage people to play games at the end of the month, such as pulling sales into the end of the month or pushing them forward.

Have a Fallback Plan

In *The Great Game of Business*, Jack Stack looks at smaller incentive plans that were adapted to meet current market challenges. If you adapt a plan to consider the market, you need to have a fallback option in case the market forces make it impossible for employees to meet the incentives. My fallback plan is to use discretionary judgment on what the target incentives should be for people who went above and beyond the call of duty but just didn't get results. Obviously, I can't give out incentives that my business can't afford. If the market prevented the employee from hitting the target, I have to use my judgment to determine what the payout should be. If the employee just didn't deliver, I have to allow the failure and decide if it's a one-time thing or if the employee needs to be transitioned into a new role or maybe even out of the company.

Chapter 6 Keys

1. Your gross profit per labor dollar is the second most important key performance indicator for your business. All labor must be productive, and you must establish your labor efficiency ratio so you can hit your profit target.

2. Culture, productivity, and profitability must all live in harmony. Culture becomes extinct without profitability. Profitability becomes extinct without productivity.

3. Set wages based on the market, not on cost of living. Wages should change only on the basis of market forces or on performance, such as moving to a new level.

4. Evaluate talent based on productivity, not on years of experience.

5. Use performance appraisals to set honest expectations of your employees and give them real feedback. Identify the top three to five core competencies you need for each role in your business.

6. Know what numbers you can share and defend, or just keep your books closed.

7. Design incentive plans that guarantee net profit increases. Forecast the financial impact of incentive plan payouts, and have a fallback plan in case the market changes.

CHAPTER 7

THE THREE SOURCES OF CAPITAL: HOW TO GET MONEY AND EFFORT TO PLAY NICELY

Each has a price; choose wisely and know the reasons for your choice.

There's tremendous confusion about the word *capital*. Simply stated, it's the difference between what you own (your assets) and what you owe (your liabilities). Another term for capital is *equity*. The capital in your business is used to purchase assets, such as inventory and equipment, and allows you to have the proper amount of cash on hand to meet your core capital target, which we discussed in chapter 4.

You can invest in a company by buying its stock, and you should expect a return on your investment. You should expect to get dividends with a nice rate of return, or you expect that the business will be sold and your investment will be worth much more than it was when you purchased the stock. When other people invest in your business, they expect the same returns on their investments.

The media interviews business owners who say things like, "I just need access to capital. I don't understand why the banks won't lend to me." Here's where the confusion arises: *debt is not capital*! Sometimes you'll hear the term *borrowed capital*, but that's an extreme distortion because capital isn't the same as debt. Those are two different things. It's either debt or capital.

When you have debt, the lenders love their money more than they love your business. It's just a plain and simple fact. They're in it for the return on their money. Remember that a loan must be repaid, and the terms are very inflexible. Banks have the worst timing when it comes to repaying loans. They want to collect when they think you are at risk, which is when you have the least ability to repay. At the moment they're probably being more lenient than they should be, which could be detrimental to their own businesses. There are so many troubled businesses that banks are unwilling to create a cascade of losses by closing everyone down.

Certainly, there are times when you can use term debt (a fixed-payment note that is repaid over an agreed period of time) as a bridge to give you time to build capital through retaining profits in the business. If you build a bridge by getting a term note because you don't have enough capital in your business, you have to make sure you make enough profit to get you over that bridge and to the other side of the river before the bridge collapses. In most cases, bankers are not going to be forgiving if you don't make it to the other side of the river. It's not that they're evil; it's what their business is built to do.

There is a lot of flexibility with the way financial problems are working out at the moment, but there is also a lot of trepidation among entrepreneurs who are unsure of the future. Some people are fully drawn on lines of credit, and they can't make a payment. I have clients who are struggling, and they don't know if their bank is going to allow them to convert their line of credit into a term note and start making payments to pay down the principal or if the bank is going to pull the loan and foreclose.

You should keep all this in mind when you decide how you'll obtain capital. You have three choices: your own money, other people's money, and sweat equity. Each one has its price. Choose wisely and know the reasons for your choice.

SOURCE #1: USE YOUR OWN MONEY

Early in my career, a client of mine wanted to start a business with no debt, so we sat down and calculated exactly what his capital requirements would be. When he left, he realized that he was $40,000 short of what was required. He said, "Thanks. I'm not going to start it yet, but

I know how I'll get $40,000." He owned a piece of land, and he sold it for $40,000 to get his capital. He started his business with no debt and never borrowed a dime. He didn't borrow against his land; he did the sure thing so he wouldn't have debt hanging over his head. Instead of looking to the banks, your mom, or the SBA, look at your own resources and see if you can avoid debt.

It seems like a novel concept to use your own money to start your own business, but it's possible and it has been done. If you start a business with your own money, you're going to defend it to the greatest degree. It's unlike anything else because you're the most frugal when it is your own money. You had to work hard to get it, so you're going to be careful with it. I've seen people inherit money and totally blow it. That money wasn't earned, and that's the difference. When people invest money they earned, it's very precious and they're careful with it.

When you capitalize your business with your own money, you want a good return on your investment. You can calculate it by dividing your pretax profit by your equity. As you know, my philosophy is that your business should make somewhere between 10 and 15 percent pretax profit. That rate of profitability coupled with maintaining a core capital target of two months of operating expenses with nothing drawn on a line of credit works out to about a 40 to 50 percent rate of return on the investment that you have in the business. When you get beyond 15 percent profitability, the return goes up to about 60 to 70 percent.

Remember Company B from our black hole example in chapter 3? Exhibit 7.1 shows their return on investment. You can see that over time their capital grew, and so did their distributions. The return-on-investment percentage is higher in the first two years because the company still had some debt to fund their receivables, but it normalized in the last three years when there was no debt in the company. This is where you can be fooled by percentages. Your return-on-investment percentage can be higher if you use debt, but you are adding risk to the business that prevents it from surviving hard times. Yes, it flies higher, but it also hits the ground harder when it falls.

Exhibit 7.1: Return on Investment Example					
	Year 1	Year 2	Year 3	Year 4	Year 5
Revenue	$1,750,000	#3,200,000	$3,450,000	$4,750,000	$5,000,000
Pretax Profit	$200,000	$500,000	$415,000	$750,000	$620,000
% to Income	11.4%	15.6%	12.0%	15.8%	12.4%
Equity	$245,000	$650,000	$ 850,000	$1,500,000	$1,300,000
Return on Investment	82%	77%	49%	50%	48%
Distribution		$95,000	$215,000	$100,000	$820,000

Unfortunately, a lot of people who have the passion for business are stuck working for somebody else, and they don't make enough money to save it for their own business venture. So what do you do if you don't have the money? Tap into your network.

SOURCE #2: OTHER PEOPLE'S MONEY

Remember the graph in exhibit 3.10 that showed the pretax profit line going straight up and the breakeven point in twenty-one months? These kinds of cases can't be totally funded with debt. You have to find some partners who are going to be patient, long-term investors, or you have to be patient and grow only at the rate of your profitability increase. Take your pick, because those are your only two choices. As a general rule, I recommend other people's money (OPM) as the funding source of last resort. If you don't have enough money to do it right, then wait until you do.

With OPM, you're not as careful because it's not your money. Until you burn through all that money, you don't make the hard choices that you should have made back when you first got the money. I can count on one hand how many of my clients have taken OPM and diligently protected that cash as a precious resource. Interestingly enough, every one of those clients came from very meager beginnings. They knew what it was like to experience scarcity, and they never wanted to go back there again.

When you use OPM, you have to be clear about the investors' expectations and let them know you're not giving them a salary. They get a salary only if they do a particular job within the business operation.

The more sophisticated the investor, the more reasonable the expectations and the tougher the terms of the deal. Investors with experience have lost enough times to know which questions to ask and which provisions to place in the agreement to protect their investment. It's certainly dangerous to have investors with high expectations. They think they're going to give you $20,000 and it's going to turn into $20 million. This scenario has happened before, but it's highly unlikely. It's just as bad for somebody to give you $50,000 and have zero expectations. I've seen this situation over and over again. Usually it happens because the business goals weren't clearly stated. The business drifts along and then a lot of time passes and no one is really paying attention. It's almost like the investors have forgotten about you.

In setting expectations, you have to play out three scenarios. The scenario we all enjoy is when everything goes great and you can either sell the business to the highest bidder or keep operating the business and harvest the cash flow. The next scenario is quite common. The business gets stuck at some point without having reached its goals, so it needs more investment money to push through. In the last scenario, the business is just surviving and the owner is happy to live off it with no possible return for the investors. Unfortunately, the last scenario is the most common, and it's the death of the business. You tried, failed, and it is time to close the doors. If there are any assets of value left during the shutdown, you have to decide who gets preference when it comes to returning investment money. Does it go to the owners or the investors?

You can get OPM from three sources: friends, family, and fools; angel investors; or venture capitalists.

Friends, Family, and Fools

Friends, family, and fools are the most common sources of OPM because when you calculate the amount of capital that's needed to start a business, it's usually less than $100,000—in many cases, it's less than $50,000. This isn't a lot of money in terms of building a business, so this amount is usually within reach of friends, family, and fools.

You have to keep in mind that with this approach, your investors will have either unrealistically high expectations or no expectations at all. You can have really bad consequences if the deal goes bad. You lose friends. You become estranged from family members. And fools have a tendency to be quite litigious (so do some family members!). There are endless lawsuits because no one set clear expectations, and everyone ends up with their noses out of joint. This is why legal agreements should be drafted by an experienced attorney (not cousin Vinnie who just got out of law school). Legal documents will not keep you from having a dispute, but they will make a difference in the speed of the settlement.

Angel Investors

Angel investors are a great source for capital. They are accredited by the Securities and Exchange Commission as having $1 million of net worth, excluding their personal residence. Angel investors are individuals, not venture capital firms. They typically have active businesses and do angel investing only as a side activity. It's a lot more structured now than it was twenty to thirty years ago.

Most angels invest between $20,000 and $1 million, but the sweet spot is $50,000 to $100,000. As I said before, the majority of my clients build businesses on $100,000 or less. You can find local angels by connecting with the local business community through the chamber of commerce and networking at local entrepreneurial events. Angels are usually easy to find because many of them like to tell stories of their good deals. Occasionally, they will also tell stories of the ones that did not work.

I strongly urge you to research the track record of angels to see how they handle the ups and downs. They have probably been part of some bad deals, and how they handled those situations is a predictor of how they'll react when things go sour. You also want to set expectations with angel investors. They probably have a little longer fuse, but eventually they'll put some pressure on you. On the other hand, some angels have let deals go on for many, many years, so it's hard to predict.

More times than not, angels will push you to sign agreements. Unfortunately, some angels get a little sloppy because they don't like to pay legal fees, so they start doing unprofessional documentation of their expectations and agreements. If you don't have enough money to hire professional legal assistance, then you don't have enough money to do the deal. It's as simple as that.

Venture Capitalists

Venture capitalists (VCs) are similar to angels except investing is their primary business activity. If you want to build a business to sell, obtaining venture capital is the fastest way. Since it is their business, VCs want to make enough money to compensate for their time and the money they invest, so they tend to move *upstream*. That is, they target businesses valued at $10 million or more. In weak markets they will move downstream a little bit or take a chance on an early-stage company that has really high potential. In most cases, the source of the VC's money is either personal accumulated wealth or someone else's money.

VCs probably deserve both the good and bad things that have been written about them. You have to go into a relationship with a VC with your eyes wide open and understand their expectations. They are professional investors and demand a return on their money. They want revenue, demonstrable profitability, and growth. When VCs invest on behalf of other people, they don't want to get beaten up by their clients.

If you don't deliver, they may either run you out of your own business or sell your business. There's no in-between. If your business value doesn't go up, they'll get out.

SOURCE #3: SWEAT EQUITY

Sweat equity is probably the most common source of capital, and it's my favorite. There's something so American and entrepreneurial about rubbing two dollar bills together to make a profit. Even if I had money of my own to put into a business, I would preserve my cash and use sweat equity before I'd use my own cash or someone else's.

Sweat equity is the least understood and least measured form of capital. I've made a practice of bringing it to the forefront to help people understand why it exists. It's all about your effort and hard work. If you can't afford to pay yourself a market-based wage for your efforts, then you're going to have to defer payment and work for it. Structure your life so you can live on little or no salary until you can afford to pay yourself a better wage, and remember that even if you can pay yourself only a $20,000 salary, that doesn't mean that's all you're worth.

As we discussed in chapter 1, the trap that most people fall into is believing that because they have a low wage, they can live off the profits of the business. It's better to live off your savings and let your sweat equity build capital in your business. Then pay yourself a market-based wage when your business reaches 2 or 3 percent pretax profit.

Suppose you started your business for $100,000 and your market-based wage should be $75,000 per year. You can create equity by working for no wages in year one, pay yourself $50,000 in year two, and be at a full wage in year three. That just created $100,000 of capital! You can supplement your salary with your savings during the first two years. I find that pulling money from savings to live on creates the most focus for entrepreneurs.

Exchanging Sweat Equity for Stock

In chapter 1 I talked about a scenario when there are two owners in a business and only one can go without wages and give sweat equity. There has to be some type of agreement to settle up the differences. Actually, this forces you into a good situation because you have to recognize the value of the business so you can set up an exchange of some kind to make up for the difference in contribution from the two owners.

My preference, in this situation, is that stock changes hands at least every year. Let's say John and Mary started a business, and they are equal shareholders. John can't live without a salary of $100,000 a year, but Mary, who is just as valuable as he is, needs to make only $50,000 a year. If John keeps booking $50,000 a year for four years, then John owes Mary $200,000. To their dismay—especially Mary's—the business doesn't look like it's going to be able to repay the $200,000. John let four years of life go by before making the hard decisions that should have been made four years earlier. Not only that, but Mary made a bad investment by taking sweat equity.

If you settle up on the stock differential, it creates focus and draws attention to the business. Mary, who was making $50,000 but was worth $100,000, should have owned a greater percentage of the company instead of only 50 percent, and John would have seen some changes in her behavior. It's as simple as that. If Mary had received additional stock each year as she went without full pay, I guarantee you the hard decisions about business performance would have been made sooner.

Exchanging Sweat Equity for Ownership

The most common sweat equity arrangement is when someone wants to earn their way into a business. Let's say Patrick is one of your key employees and you want him to be an owner of the business. You have an incentive program whereby he can make up to $50,000 in extra income per year. At the end of the year, Patrick made the bonus, but unfortunately the IRS has to get their Social Security, Medicare, and payroll taxes. It's too bad, but Patrick won't net $50,000. He'll get $50,000 gross minus 40 percent in taxes, which leaves him with $30,000.

Let's say you put that $30,000 on the table in front of Patrick, and you tell him that, before he picks up the money, you have a *better* deal for him. You say, "You know the business is worth $750,000. And IRS rules allow me to use a discount for lack of marketability because we are a closely held business. And since you have less than a controlling interest in the business, I can discount it." That discount averages somewhere between 40 and 45 percent. So if you have 750,000 shares and it's worth $750,000, you can offer Patrick a dollar a share. But you can give him an opportunity to buy at $0.60 a share since you are allowed to discount it under the IRS rules.

Patrick knows you have a really good business because you practice OBM and he's seen the numbers. You bring in $1 million of revenue per year and, as a top-performing business, you make a 15 percent pretax profit of $150,000. You've met your core capital target (two months of operating expenses in cash with nothing drawn on a line of credit), so you don't have any debt. Patrick can see the percentage of stock that he could own and that he could get a distribution of profits. Exhibit 7.2 shows how the math works out.

Exhibit 7.2 Sweat Equity Bonus Example			
Bonus (assume base pay of $ 75,000)		$50,000	
Social Security and Medicare		($2,697)	5.39 %
Federal & State Withholding (est.)		($17,302)	34.61 %
Net Check Used to Purchase % of the Business		$30,000	
After 40% Discount			
Annual Revenue	$1,000,000		
Average Pretax Profit	$150,000		
Equity	$300,000		
(core capital of $150,000 plus receivables of $150,000)			

Business Value (Average Pretax profit x 3) + (Equity)	$750,000	$750,000	$450,000
Current Shares Outstanding	$1 = $750,000/$750,000		
Current Shares Outstanding	$0.60 = $450,000/$750,000		
Current Shares Outstanding	$750,000		
Shares Purchased for $30,000 net	$50,000		
Total Shares Outstanding	$800,000		

ROI	Annual Profit	% Ownership	Investment	ROI	Tax Distribution	Profit Distribution
Original SH	$140,625	93.75%	$300,000	46%	$56,250	$84,375
Patrick	$9,375	6.25%	$30,000	31%	$3,750	$5,625

Patrick purchases stock using his $30,000 net bonus. He can't use the gross amount of $50,000 because taxes have to be paid. With the discount, Patrick uses his $30,000 to buy shares at $0.60 a share, which gives him 50,000 shares ($30,000 divided by $0.60 = 50,000 shares). With 800,000 total shares, his 50,000 shares give him 6.25 percent ownership of the business. With $150,000 of pretax profit, his 6.25 percent ownership gives him a profit allocation of $9,375 (150,000 x 0.0625). That $9,375 is taxable, so he's going to owe 40 percent, or $3,750, in taxes. If I make a $30,000 investment and make interest income off of it, the interest income I make is taxable. So, it's an equivalent factor. I owe the bonus to Patrick one way or the other. Patrick can choose to use his after-tax earnings to buy stock in the business to get future returns that will potentially be greater than the net pay he could get by taking the bonus.

To make this a real investment, it must not affect Patrick's salary. He has paid a fair amount for his shares, and he is due a fair return (notice his ROI is still less than yours!). You started the business and get an ROI closer to 50 percent. This is because you bought it when it wasn't worth $1 million; it was worth $200,000 to $300,000. This shows how, as a business grows over time, the rate of return on the money you leave in the business will continue to grow as well.

Patrick gets an ROI of 31 percent (9,375 ÷ 30,000) in a business that he knows. Not only that, he becomes a member of the team and gets to be involved in decision-making processes. What he has to decide, though, is if he wants to be a shareholder or not. Does he believe that he'll continue to receive a 31 percent rate of return on his money? He must decide if this is a good way to invest his $30,000 or if he'd rather have the cash. If he picks the money up off the table, you know Patrick just wants the income. If he doesn't pick it up, he not only wants to buy into the economic engine, but he also wants to be part of the ownership structure and build a more valuable future.

Granted, there are people who want to be owners for reasons that don't involve economic decisions, but I encourage my clients *not* to have those people as owners because it messes up the value of what the shares really mean. Employees who become shareholders should be motivated first and foremost by the desire to get a return on their investment.

Chapter 7 Keys

1. Do not fall into the trap of thinking that debt is capital.

2. Save your own money whenever possible and use it to start your business.

3. If you accept investment money, you must meet the expectations of the investors. If you are unwilling to do that, don't take their money.

4. Document your investors' expectations and hire a professional lawyer to draft your shareholder agreements.

5. Put sweat equity into your business whenever possible. It will always give you the best possible return on investment.

6. Make fair sweat equity arrangements when multiple shareholders are involved.

7. Whenever employees want to earn their way into the business, make sure they are motivated by returns on their investment.

CHAPTER 8

REPORTING RHYTHMS: THE RIGHT DATA AT THE RIGHT TIME

Your numbers are talking . . . are you listening?

Getting into a reporting rhythm is often a challenge for entrepreneurs. They struggle to know what reports they're supposed to look at, when they're supposed to look at them, and why they're supposed to look at them.

Looking at reports is kind of like looking at the dashboard of a car. The problem with dashboards is they can have too many gauges and indicators. The information you want is there, but you don't know where to look for it. If you try to track too many numbers and create too much data, you end up with your own version of a busy dashboard. You have to know how to keep your reporting simple while still being able to recognize a flashing red light that indicates a problem.

When I work with a client who's trying to look at the business in a different way, the first thing I establish is a reporting rhythm. We decide what data we need to support that rhythm as well as how important the information is to managing the business. For instance, is a particular number just a good thing to know, or is it something that says you need to take action if it's above or below a specified number? Have you set action triggers at the right points, or are you being too soft on your requirements?

If you're going to look at a report frequently, it needs to show a very small amount of data. If you're going to look at it infrequently, it can contain more data. Don't fool yourself into thinking that a one-page report is a small amount of data. You can use a small font and use every bit of white space until it can't be read by the human eye. The report has to be easy to read and digest; otherwise it won't be useful.

A lot of entrepreneurs say they don't need to see a report if the numbers are already in QuickBooks. Just because numbers are in Quick-Books doesn't mean you're going to look at them. I don't know any entrepreneurs who have the discipline to look in QuickBooks every time they need to answer a question. You have to push critical data into a report and read it. I don't care whether you read it electronically or kill a tree and print it, just read it. You can delegate the preparation, but it's still your responsibility to make sure it gets prepared. There are people in my office who prepare the critical reports, but it still falls on me to say, "Hey, I was supposed to get a report today. Where is it?"

Let's take a look at what reports you need in your reporting rhythm and how we can keep the numbers speaking to you:

1. Daily report: Cash balance

2. Weekly reports: Cash flow forecast; sales and productivity

3. Monthly reports: Profit and loss; balance sheet and where the cash goes

DAILY REPORT: CASH BALANCE

You'd be surprised at how many entrepreneurs have no clue about how much cash they have in their business on a given day. Even though you might not be as involved in the day-to-day processing as you used to be, you can process this information in a very short period of time. I like the daily cash balance report to include which customers paid and what the cash balance is after today's deposit. Once you get beyond about twenty customers, listing who paid is not always practical, but you would still report the total deposit for the day and the cash balance. An example of a cash balance report is shown in exhibit 8.1. It is important to note that this report needs to be simple and easy to e-mail and read on a PDA or smart phone without opening an attachment.

Exhibit 8.1 Daily Cash Balance Report	
Customer payments:	
Bob's Auto Repair	$2,000.00
XYZ Engineering	$1,500.00
Fred and Mary Smith	$750.00
Total Deposit	$4,250.00
QB Cash Balance	$82,652.71

Believe it or not, there is some dispute over how to arrive at how much cash you have. My definition of cash balance is the bank balance in your accounting system, assuming all outstanding checks have cleared. If your bookkeeper tells you he or she cannot produce this because the cash balance in your accounting system is not up to date, that is a key indicator you have a big problem. Have that person fix it or get a new bookkeeper. Someone in your office can be trained to send this report in a daily e-mail to the key people in your business. If you use a program such as QuickBooks, you can e-mail the amount of the deposit from within the software. You don't even have to retype it.

No matter where I am in the world, I get a daily e-mail that tells me who paid us that day and what the cash balance is. That may sound like basic information, but it really does matter. I can see if a long-overdue bill was paid and who pays their bills on time. If the cash balance is low, it tells me to have a great sense of urgency to solve the problem. If it's high, it tells me all is good.

When Jack Stack and his management team bought Springfield Re-Manufacturing, they considered the cash balance to be a critical number, and they posted it above the time clock in all of their facilities. Their mission was to avoid running out of cash. They bought their business for $9 million, and they borrowed $8.9 million of it. Rumor has it that the banker who loaned them the money was fired shortly afterward for making bad loans to companies like them, so they knew that if they ever went into default, they had no advocate at the bank. They simply could not afford to miss a payment. The tricky part is that they didn't make any profit in the first year. How did they survive and not miss a payment? They sold everything they didn't need, including excess inventory and anything that wasn't bolted down. They generated cash any possible way they could. The next year they were profitable.

WEEKLY REPORTS

Create a rhythm by sticking to whatever day of the week works for you to review your weekly reports. You should look at two reports every week: cash flow forecast and sales and production. It should take a clerk-level person (your controller's productivity shouldn't be wasted on this easy task) about fifteen minutes to pull the data together if it's properly recorded in the first place.

Cash Flow Forecast Report

The purpose of the cash flow forecast report is to make sure you have money in the bank when your bills are due. It shows a two-week projection of your expected sources of inflows and outflows. Break your payables up into these five key categories:

- General bills
- Payroll
- Payroll taxes and benefits
- Rent
- Payments for debt (lines of credit and fixed-term notes)

You may have one or two more categories, but these five are the most common. The key is to make sure you don't have a long list. In my firm, one thing we add at the bottom of our list is a running total of partner paychecks that have been missed. If we run out of cash, the owners forgo compensation so that everyone else can get paid. If you miss a paycheck instead of drawing on a line of credit, it gets you focused real quick so you make sure the payroll gets back on track. You do deserve a paycheck, but only if the business is profitable and you're not having to draw on a line of credit.

Exhibit 8.2 is an example of a cash flow forecast report.

Exhibit 8.2: CASH FLOW FORECAST For the week ending 5/22/20XX				
	ABC Bank	**XYZ Bank**	**Total**	
QB Balance:	$ 71,338.98	$ 25,000.00	$ 96,338.98	
Total Line	$ 100,000.00			
LOC Balance	$ 25,000.00			
Available for draw	$ 75,000.00			
Accounts Receivable:				
0-30	31–60	61–90	> 90	TOTAL
$ 84,375.30	$ 10,645.90	$ 19,063.00	$ 65,853.80	$ 179,938.00
Payables		**5/25/20XX**	**6/1/20XX**	
	Bills	$ 6,912.52	$ 738.59	
	Credit Card Payables	$ 1,013.25	$ 525.00	
	Loan Payment (1st)		$ 2,500.00	
	Rent (1st)	$ 9,935.00		
	Tax Deposit		$ 8,930.94	
	Payroll (Net)	$ 26,002.24		
	401(k)		$ 1,548.65	
		$ 43,863.01	$ 14,243.18	

Let's say today's cash balance report shows $50,000, and this week's cost and cash flow report shows you have only $10,000 in bills to pay this week. It looks good until you see that next week you need to cover a $50,000 payroll. The cash flow forecast report spurs you into action, and you look at what receivables you need to collect so you can make the payroll next week. Maybe you have to make other arrangements, such as drawing against your line of credit. You have time to think about a solution because you have a two-week advance warning that there's a problem. A few of my clients tried to expand the projection beyond two weeks with limited success. This report is designed to give you a two-week heads-up about your cash flow.

My firm pays bills on Mondays, which means that on Fridays we're making sure that everything that needs to be paid is in the system. Before the checks go out the door, this report gives me a snapshot of our cash balance, aged receivables, and who needs to be paid. We don't use a lot of credit because we don't believe in supporting our business that way, but if you need to use your line of credit to cover your payables, look at how much it is, what you've drawn on it, and what's still available.

Here's a question I always ask in my entrepreneur classes: What does the "due date" field in QuickBooks mean to you? Most of the class says it's the date that people want the bill to be paid by. Wrong. That date tells me which Monday to get the check in the mail. Since we pay bills only on Mondays, we have to mail checks on the Monday before the due date so they get to the vendors on time. I can use that field however I want, so it works with my payment processing procedures.

Sales and Productivity Report

I'm not a fan of measuring sales on a daily basis unless you are a retail business or you invoice daily. It creates that busy dashboard we talked about earlier. Even with retail clients who have daily sales, I look at sales on a week-to-week basis because it gives me better numbers overall.

Recently I've successfully tied labor efficiency to weekly sales. Remember, labor efficiency is gross profit per labor dollar. For example, I was able to determine a client's gross profit before any labor was taken out by basically taking their sales minus their cost of goods sold. Let's say that gross profit before labor came out to 50 percent of sales, so if they had a $40,000 sales week, they had $20,000 in *nonlabor gross margin*, which is our term for the cost of gross profit before any labor is taken out.

The client's goal was to have a labor efficiency of 2.0. So that week's payroll needed to be $10,000. Their production was equal to what their labor productivity should have been. Keep in mind that's *all* labor—not just production labor, but also the office staff and everyone else. If their payroll had been $12,000, it would have been higher than what their labor efficiency should have been. The client would have had to ask if that was a one-week anomaly or if it's something that needed to be tracked.

The best practice seems to be watching this on a weekly basis and then looking at it month-to-date and year-to-date to see if the trends move in the right direction. Exhibit 8.3 is an example of a labor productivity report. You can go to my firm's website (www.seeingbeyondnumbers .com) to download a copy of the spreadsheet so you can see how the formulas work.

Exhibit 8.3: Sales and Productivity Report							
						Labor Efficiency Ratio	
Period	GP%	Sales	GP$	Cost of Labor	Week	MTD	YTD
January	49.50%	$145,000	$71,775	$35,000		$2.05	$2.05
February	51.20%	$154,000	$78,848	$37,000		$2.13	$2.09
March	47.60%	$180,000	$85,680	$40,000		$2.14	$2.11
April	50.10%	$190,000	$95,190	$42,000		$2.27	$2.15
May							
Week 1	50.00%	$40,000	$20,000	$10,000	$2.00	$2.00	$2.14
Week 2	50.00%	$38,000	$19,000	$9,500	$2.00	$2.00	$2.14
Week 3	50.00%	$35,000	$17,500	$11,000	$1.59	$1.85	$2.10
Week 4	50.00%					$1.85	$2.10
Week 5	50.00%					$1.85	$2.10
May Total		$113,000	$56,500	$30,500		$1.85	$2.10

After we identify what your labor efficiency ratio is (that is, your gross profit per labor dollar), that number won't change dramatically once your business model is set. When you look at chains with great labor management, such as Outback and Starbucks, you'll find that they send a $9-per-hour person home early when productivity drops below a certain level. That way, they won't have to make up the $20-plus in revenue the next day to cover the cost of keeping the $9-per-hour employee on duty.

You need to understand the pulse of your business. The Outbacks of the world manage their numbers on an hourly basis, but if you manage yours on at least a weekly basis, you'll start to establish a gut feeling about the numbers. If you don't have a natural gut feeling, you can develop it by watching the two numbers that matter most: gross profit and cost of labor. That's it! And if you don't understand that part, your business model is never going to work.

MONTHLY REPORTS

Pick a day of the month to review your monthly reports. Don't look at them every day, or you'll become blind to the numbers. On your chosen day of the month, pull the numbers together or delegate the task to someone else. Spend time looking at the numbers and determine if your money is being well spent or if you need to make changes. If you are not getting these key reports by the fifth of the month, you need to find the bottleneck and eliminate it.

Profit and Loss Report: Monthly and Rolling Twelve

A profit and loss report (P&L) shows you if your business made or lost money during the reporting period. It shows your revenue, costs, and expenses, and it concludes with your net income. You just have to keep in mind that a month is an extremely inaccurate period of time. I'd never look at just one month by itself; I'd look at a minimum of six months of monthly data to see what the ups and downs were. The most useful presentation of the P&L for me is a rolling-twelve view.

Put simply, a rolling-twelve view of a P&L shows every month ending a twelve-month accounting period. When you compare the twelve-month periods side by side, you start to see more of a macro view of your business. When you graph that data, you can see the true trends of the business and answer questions like: What's my overall revenue? What's my gross profit? What's my salary cap? Since you're monitoring rolling-twelve data, you can't excuse numbers because of a particular season. Rolling-twelve data filters out all the excuses because the data has been through four seasons and includes every holiday. If you see that you had some hiccups during a twelve-month period of time, you can determine if you can avoid those same hiccups in the future.

If you have a P&L that's two pages long with multiple line items, your eyes are going to roll back into your head and you'll want to just let your accountant deal with it. You can't abdicate that role. You have to understand and be responsible for your data. Continuously refine the report to make sure you're looking at data that's valuable to you. If you find that some numbers aren't helpful, then quit reporting them. That's really the key to a useful report.

Keep the top level of your P&L very thin; that is, only seven or eight lines of data, not including subtitles. For instance, with a revenue presentation, if I sell both products and services, I would show revenue from each. If my cost of goods sold has a labor component and a goods component, I definitely have to separate those because I have to do calculations with the labor number.

An example of a rolling-twelve P&L is shown in exhibit 8.4. This represents only six months of data for illustrative purposes, but you should include at least twelve months or more in your report. Remember, each column represents twelve months of data. The first column covers the twelve months ended in December, the second column covers the twelve months ended in January, and so on. Essentially, each month you are adding the new month and dropping the same month from the previous year.

In exhibit 8.4, you can see the company was struggling for the twelve months ended December because their pretax profit was below target and they needed to increase their productivity. They had two choices: reduce

Exhibit 8.4: Rolling-Twelve P&L

	20X1-12	20X2-01	20X2-02	20X2-03	20X2-04	20X2-05	20X2-06
Revenue	815,000.00	950,000.00	970,000.00	1,008,000.00	998,000.00	1,085,000.00	1,120,000.00
Cost of Goods Sold	289,000.00	315,000.00	320,000.00	320,000.00	315,000.00	322,000.00	320,000.00
Gross Profit	526,000.00	635,000.00	650,000.00	688,000.00	683,000.00	763,000.00	800,000.00
as % to Revenue	65%	67%	67%	68%	68%	70%	71%
Operating Expenses:							
Labor - All	369,000.00	384,000.00	391,000.00	394,000.00	405,000.00	408,000.00	418,000.00
Marketing	48,000.00	52,000.00	53,000.00	53,000.00	50,000.00	49,000.00	48,000.00
Facilities	74,000.00	79,000.00	78,000.00	80,000.00	87,000.00	90,000.00	89,000.00
Payroll taxes & benefits	31,000.00	32,000.00	33,000.00	42,000.00	43,000.00	45,000.00	46,000.00
Other operating expenses	72,000.00	81,000.00	87,000.00	100,000.00	101,000.00	97,000.00	93,000.00
Total Operating Expenses	594,000.00	628,000.00	642,000.00	669,000.00	686,000.00	689,000.00	694,000.00

Net Pretax Profit	(68,000.00)	7,000.00	8,000.00	19,000.00	(3,000.00)	74,000.00	106,000.00
as % to Revenue	-8.34%	0.74%	0.82%	1.88%	-0.30%	6.82%	9.46%
Pretax Profit target @ 10%	81,500.00	95,000.00	97,000.00	100,800.00	99,800.00	108,500.00	112,000.00
Above (below) target	(149,500.00)	(88,000.00)	(89,000.00)	(81,800.00)	(102,800.00)	(34,500.00)	(6,000.00)
Salary Cap	219,500.00	296,000.00	302,000.00	312,200.00	302,200.00	373,500.00	412,000.00
Labor efficiency (GP/Labor$)	1.43	1.65	1.66	1.75	1.69	1.87	1.91
Labor efficiency target @ 10% pretax profit	2.40	2.15	2.15	2.20	2.26	2.04	1.94
Additional GP needed to hit 15% pretax profit							62,000.00
Productivity increase required							8%

labor by $149,500 annually or increase their labor productivity to generate $149,500 more in revenue without hiring any additional labor. They chose to swap out a couple of staff members, but they mostly kept the same level of labor expense and increased their labor productivity through management and leadership. Once they had a target to aim for, they pushed through the hard-to-do things to hit it. This gave them a 6 percent increase in gross profit as a percentage of revenue along with a $300,000 increase in revenue. At the end of June, they had recovered to a pretax profit of 10 percent. You can see that if they had cut labor, the labor efficiency required would have been $2.40, which would have been too steep a cut in their case to remain viable. Once they grew to almost $1 million in revenue, the amount leveled out to just above $2.00. My counsel to this client was to get to 15 percent pretax profit before they tried to grow significantly past $1 million in revenue. Note that this growth required only $62,000 of additional gross profit, which equated to an 8 percent increase in productivity from their existing staff. I would rather see them generate 8 percent more through productivity than think they can squeeze 8 percent out of their operating expenses.

In exhibit 8.4, this company sold only services, so they only had one line of revenue presented. I left direct labor out of cost of goods sold and showed all labor in the operating expense section. You can see there is no one standard way of showing the P&L presentation. The key is to be consistent and make it meaningful to you.

In general, the operating expenses settle into the following five categories:

1. Labor

2. Marketing

3. Facilities

4. Payroll taxes and benefits

5. Other operating expenses

Labor

Remember how important your salary cap is? With your labor expense number, you can see what your salary cap is and how it relates to labor. For instance, if we can calculate that you're at 5 percent profitability, we can tell you what your salary cap *should have been* for you to be at 10 percent profitability, so you can track your labor trends compared to what your salary cap *should* be.

When you see that, you truly start to understand the ebbs and flows of your business. I've done this historical analysis for many entrepreneurs, and most of them can look at each month and tell you exactly where they got lax and forgot to manage their business. They can also tell you exactly when they stopped accepting excuses for why certain things were happening. You can see in exhibit 8.5 (this is the same data we showed in exhibit 8.4, only in graph form) where they made hard decisions and the business started to turn and build up again.

If you see a rolling twelve-month decline in labor productivity and the salary cap is not being met, you'll start questioning things a lot sooner. Most entrepreneurs instinctively know where the weak points are. They just need the data to support their gut feeling. As you can see in exhibit 8.5, it took this company only three months to move from break-even to almost 10 percent pretax profit.

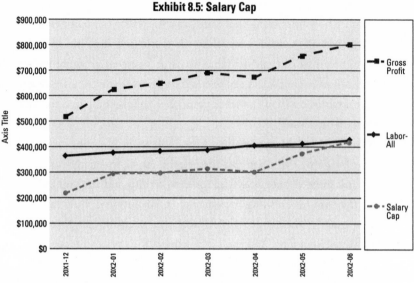

Exhibit 8.5: Salary Cap

Marketing

When companies are struggling to get beyond the $1 million mark, they usually starve their marketing budget because they don't have a strategy about how to spend the dollars and they don't see an immediate impact from the dollars they do spend. They often don't have a gut-level feel for what to expect for their marketing dollars. In the franchise world, the recommendation is to spend a minimum of 2 to 5 percent of your revenue on marketing. Even if you get customers from one-on-one networking, you still have to spend marketing dollars on collateral materials, like brochures. Budget between 2 and 5 percent for marketing, but continually monitor if it's working and if you're getting value from the marketing. Get a better grasp on how to strategically spend the dollars.

Facilities

I include rent, repairs and maintenance, IT costs, and communications costs in my definition of facilities expenses. Even though some of these costs vary each month, you will be surprised by how little they move.

Payroll Taxes and Benefits

This category is broken out separately because it is the one cost that moves in direct proportion to your labor cost. It includes all payroll taxes, health and disability insurance, workers' compensation insurance, and any other fringe benefits. If this line item does not move in proportion to labor, it needs to be investigated.

Other Operating Expenses

This is the catchall category for all other costs that do not fit in the other categories. Once again, this category is very consistent each month and will spike only a couple of times each year. As you look back over the previous one to two years, you should easily be able to predict when the spikes will occur and what the drivers are.

Quick Tips About QuickBooks

There are some great features in QuickBooks for producing P&L statements. You can set roll-up points for your key seven or eight lines of data we talked about earlier, then you can expand them for more detail or collapse them to see just those seven or eight lines. First look at the collapsed view across time and see if there are any anomalies. If you see something interesting, expand it so you can drill down to the underlying cause of the movement.

Unfortunately, QuickBooks doesn't have the ability to produce a rolling twelve-month P&L or month-to-month rolling-twelve data. I wish it did, because it would be a fabulous feature for reporting purposes. If possible, hire someone to update the model you're using so you can quickly access the data. Otherwise just use a spreadsheet and continue to look for ways to improve the process. For businesses under $5 million, I often have to cobble together data from many different sources through spreadsheets or databases, then I find ways for them to maintain or automate the data effectively and efficiently for future reporting.

Where Cash Goes (Hint: It Requires You to Know How to Read a Balance Sheet)

One of the biggest challenges that entrepreneurs face is trying to understand if their data is based on cash-based or accrual-based accounting. QuickBooks does have the ability to produce a balance sheet and P&L based on the cash-basis method, but it contains some distortions. You have to book the information in exactly the right way for the cash-basis presentation to be accurate. I've never seen a truly accurate cash-basis balance sheet and P&L produced with this software.

You need to understand accrual-basis accounting so you'll know where the cash is coming from and where it's going to go. For instance, when are your receivables going to turn into cash? That tells you where your inflows are coming from. If you know what your payables are, that tells you when your money has to go out. You can also see what the terms are and if you can rely on your vendors for trade support. You'll begin to understand that the connection is the balance sheet. Your P&L does report a sale, but if you don't have the money yet, it's sitting over there on the balance sheet as a receivable. And as I'm fond of saying, all the dead bodies are on the balance sheet. It reveals the errors in your books. If you find a number on the balance sheet that is incorrectly presented, your P&L is just as worthless as the balance sheet. You have to fix your balance sheet to get your P&L right.

The simple rule of accounting is this: If your balance sheet is right at the beginning of a period and it's right at the end of the period, then the net income number has to be right. It's a closed system; it has to work. So if you find an error, don't continue to explain it month after month. If inventory is misstated, fix it. If there's a receivable on the books that you're not going to collect, write it off.

Knowing Where Your Cash Went

After you know where your cash goes on a monthly basis, you'll know whether you had profitability or a lack of profitability. You'll know if your cash funded your receivables or if the receivables provided you with cash. You'll know if you paid off some of your payables. And you'll know if you used profits to make a shareholder distribution when you should've used the money to pay taxes.

If you don't convert your profitability to the *where did the cash go* equation we described in chapter 4, you set yourself up for something that happens to entrepreneurs every day. You can have a profitable business and run out of cash. It sounds unbelievable, but it happens all the time. That means you're growing faster than your internal funds can support you. In today's marketplace, you can't assume the bank is going to bail you out. Sometimes you have to constrict your growth to the amount you can fund yourself.

For a complete set of sample monthly reports you can use to create your own reporting pattern, see my firm's website at www.seeingbeyond numbers.com.

Chapter 8 Keys

1. Find your reporting rhythm and hold your team accountable for report production.

2. It is not the quantity of data, but the right data at the right time that matters.

3. Never take your eye off your cash balance.

4. Project your cash flow over a two-week period so you can plan for shortfalls.

5. Monitor your labor productivity by watching your gross profit and your cost of labor.

6. Use rolling-twelve data to see the macro trends of your business.

7. Keep your P&L thin; look at seven or eight key lines of data.

8. Never print a P&L without looking at your balance sheet to make sure there are no glaring errors.

CHAPTER 9

ECONOMIC VALUE: HOW TO KNOW WHAT YOUR BUSINESS IS WORTH TO YOU

A profitable, cash flow–generating business is the best of both worlds; it is valuable to you whether you keep it or sell it.

You need to know the economic value of your business to know when the business is underperforming and to have a price if you're thinking about selling it. You'll try to sell it for the highest possible value, obviously, but knowing the economic value also gives you a chance to decide if you'd rather keep it than sell it. Knowing the economic value is also useful when you offer shares to an employee or ask a partner to come into the business. It helps you decide what the terms should be, such as whether it should be a sweat-equity or cash arrangement.

There are many different opinions about the best way to determine the economic value of a business. I'll cover a variety of methods in this chapter, but first I'll describe my method, which is a blend of the cash flow–generating capacity of the business and the core capital that's built up in the business to support that income generation. I'll also describe five elements that contribute to the value of your business. The chapter will conclude with examples of economic valuations of businesses.

BLENDED METHOD FOR CALCULATING ECONOMIC VALUE

My experience has shown that the economic value of a business is typically based on the last three years of pretax profit plus the equity (assets minus liabilities) in a business. This method is a blend of the earning capacity of a business and the capitalization of the business. I have found that deals rarely get done at lower value than this, and many times a total sale of the business will yield a higher number because the seller now has a better understanding of what the business is worth whether sold or not.

50/50 Shareholder Agreements

One of the most common situations that require a proper valuation with economic reality is when there are two shareholders and one decides to sell. You need a method that is fair to both the remaining shareholder and the selling shareholder, and it has to be fundable.

To start with, if I'm going to buy 100 percent of a business, the maximum amount of time that I'm willing to wait to get my money returned to me, net after tax, is around ten years. But the timeline is different with 50/50 shareholder agreements where shareholders have what's called a *mandatory buy-sell*. If I buy out the other shareholder, I want to fund the deal by giving up no more than five years of the after-tax earnings of the business.

Here's how a mandatory buy-sell works. When one shareholder initiates the 50/50 agreement that's in place, the price is set. Then the other shareholder gets to choose whether to buy or sell at that price. If I'm a 50/50 shareholder and I want my partner out of the business, I can say, "Fred, I want to buy you out. I'm going to offer you $500,000." I would immediately lose control of the agreement; Fred could say, "Well, I don't want to sell, but I accept your offer, and I'll pay you $500,000."

Within that buy-sell, I structure the agreement so the buyer can pay for it over a five-year period. The economic value of the business should be justified during that period. So if I were Fred's advisor, I'd say that if the business has enough after-tax cash flows, he should pay for the note in five years. This is a good deal, so Fred would want to be the buyer. If the business doesn't have enough cash flows, then it's a bad deal, and Fred would want to be the seller. It's as simple as that.

Earlier I said if I were going to buy 100 percent of a business, I'd wait about ten years to get my money back. In a shareholder situation, the buyer is buying only 50 percent, so the transaction should be completed in five years. Contrary to popular opinion, I believe a 50/50 arrangement is one of the best situations in business, in terms of a buy-sell agreement, if it is structured this way.

Using my blended approach, the valuation is three years of pretax profit plus equity (assets minus liabilities) at the date of valuation. That calculation takes into account not only the economic activity of the business, but also how well it is capitalized. This fits within my philosophy of how a good business should be structured. It is no coincidence that my blended approach for 50 percent of a business almost always comes out to the available after-tax cash flows over five years.

The company also needs to be debt free to work best in a 50 percent shareholder sale scenario. If you have a stream of pretax profit but you're sucking all that out through distributions and leaving the company heavily leveraged, you're eventually going to have a problem. You start creating a drag on the earnings because of all the interest expense you're paying. However, my blended method of valuation accounts for any debt in the business.

The other interesting thing about my blended methodology is that when the value is based on the business being fully capitalized as well as profitable, you create an alignment of both the new shareholders and the existing shareholders. They understand that the goal, first and foremost, is to run a profitable company.

In a lot of the transactions I've worked on, the selling shareholder wants to sell at a high value and then strip out the cash and receivables, leaving the buyer with a somewhat questionable economic engine as well as a business that's been damaged in terms of core capital. Not surprisingly, a lot of those businesses struggle because they needed to have new capital injected right after the initial sale of the business. You have to look at the elements that really make the deal work.

Economically Balanced Deals

One of my roles as an advisor is to make sure that whomever I represent gets a fair deal and the business still runs as it was intended to. This avoids a scenario where you try to get the maximum value when you sell your business, but if you stretch the value too far, the business will struggle under the new owner. Then the person who bought it will call you and say, "That really didn't turn out exactly the way you said it would. I think you misled me." Whether you did or you didn't is irrelevant because, as you know, anyone can file a lawsuit, and it happens every day. When the dollars are big enough, it doesn't matter if they're family members, friends, or your mortal enemies.

You want to be involved in deals that are economically balanced. The buyers know what they're getting, and the sellers know they're getting an accurate representation of the business. If a buyer wants to pay me more than the true economic value of the business, I'm going to say, "This is what you're buying. I hope you have the capital and the strategy to make it work." But as long as I've disclosed all the data to the buyer, that situation is perfectly fine. Just remember there are fools who overpay for businesses every day, and they will be looking for someone to blame when it goes bad.

The only time I adjust equity in a valuation is if the business has booked any assets or liabilities that are significantly over- or undervalued. I make the adjustment because that's either not an asset you can convert to cash or it's a liability that the business will have to pay someday.

If a shareholder who has been paid a market-based wage is leaving the business, you're going to hire somebody with that same wage to come do that person's job. That doesn't change the value. The only risk is being unable to find a replacement who has a similar skill set, but you can often find someone who is cheaper and more capable than the selling shareholder. As much as my entrepreneurial clients would like to think they're special, they're not. As I've said before, I have yet to meet anyone who's irreplaceable—I include myself in this characterization.

FIVE BASIC ELEMENTS OF VALUE

There are five basic elements that combine to drive the profits that are used to establish the value of your business: customers, employees, processes and know-how, core capital, and intellectual property. These elements are the essential drivers of your business because without customers, you have no sales or gross profit. Without employees, you have no one to execute the business strategy. If you have flawed processes, you either can't serve your customers or you'll have excess cost and lower profitability. Core capital gives you the financial resources to fund new activity and balance the ups and downs of the business cycle. Intellectual property can give you a competitive advantage and drive your business to an above-average profitability and protect market share.

Profitability, salary cap management, and the four forces of cash flow, which we talked about in previous chapters, are all contained in these five elements of value. Let's take a close look at each one:

- Customers: The degree of stickiness of your customers' relationships to your business makes your business much more valuable. The more you can build customer loyalty—to your business, but not to any one person in your business—the more valuable your business becomes. I have become a big fan of the book *Customer Satisfaction Is Worthless, Customer Loyalty Is Priceless* by Jeffrey Gitomer. He drives home the idea that without customers, you do not eat. Without the right customers, you cannot achieve your gross profit targets that will lead to your bottom-line profits.

- Employees: The ability of a business to attract talent, train talent, and develop a functional team is one of the key drivers of business value. As a buyer, I'm going to look at the quality of your team, and because you're selling and exiting the business, I'm going to determine if the team and culture are going to remain after you're gone. The right employees doing the right jobs give you labor efficiency that can beat your competition. Labor efficiency is the number one driver of profitability.

- Processes and know-how: If you've figured out a way to do something faster, better, and cheaper, then you've added intangible value to your business. I purposely separate this from intellectual property that is protected by patents, copyrights, or trademarks. Think of this as the road map you give your team that helps them win the race every day because they take fewer detours. Processes and know-how take raw *want to* labor and makes it even more efficient, which improves profitability even more.

- Core capital: You must have cash in the business. You also need receivables, inventory, and fixed assets. And then you have to consider the liabilities of the business. Did you borrow money? Do you have trade debt from vendors? From that standpoint, your assets net of your liabilities represent the core capital in the business. A business without core capital can miss opportunities, even when it has the other four elements. Remember, starve the cow and all you get is a barbeque dinner!

- Intellectual property: Anything that can be patented, copyrighted, or trademarked is what I refer to as intellectual property. Not every business has this type of value, but many who do have it don't take the proper steps to protect it. Intellectual property gives you a window of opportunity to achieve above-market profit and increase your business value in the event of a sale.

I need to caution you about a common distortion of your numbers that comes with intellectual property. Most people want to take amounts paid for intellectual property development, capitalize them, and put them on their balance sheet. Not every research and development project leads to success. If the research and development costs are capitalized and then found not successful, you then have a large worthless asset on your balance sheet that you must write off. In almost every example where a company tried to capitalize intellectual property development, they looked at it and realized it didn't work and it would have been better to expense the costs as they were spent. Intellectual property doesn't really form until somebody from outside the business is willing to pay for it.

Here's a common example: People who do website development feel the sting of expensing all that research and development. They think they can make their pretax profit look better if they capitalize it. In theory, that's true, but accounting rules do not allow you to book it that way. Research and development costs are supposed to be expensed as they occur. The buyer gets to book the assets (the intangible rights of software development) when they acquire them. In most cases, you're better off to just expense the research and development costs, take the hit, and move on.

RULE-OF-THUMB CALCULATIONS FOR VALUATION

You'll hear a lot about rule-of-thumb calculations for business value, such as five times EBITDA, one times revenue, two times revenue, and so on. Essentially, every rule-of-thumb calculation has potential problems. At the end of the day, no matter what rule of thumb you use, the value of a business is based on a willing (or desperate) buyer and a willing (or desperate) seller coming to an agreement.

Multiples of EBITDA

Everyone likes to pick the rule-of-thumb valuation method that fits their circumstances. If I have a business that's doing $5 million of revenue, but I've had no pretax profit or very meager amounts of pretax profit, obviously my business is not going to look very good as a multiple of EBITDA. I'm going to argue that if I could readjust my pretax profit, I'd look better.

Average buyers significantly overpay for businesses based on historical profitability. In the transactions I've been involved in, those buyers convinced themselves they could save on expenses or grow the business even though the previous owners were unable to do so. But from a cash-flow standpoint, these things rarely make sense, so you have to stick to the cash-flow value.

When using multiples of EBITDA, the flaws surface when you have a lack of earnings or a distortion of earnings due to incorrect owner salaries or discretionary expenses. Going back to the first chapter where we talked about owners' salaries, you'll distort the earnings of your business if you pay yourself too low a wage. You can also potentially distort the earnings of your business by paying yourself too high a wage. And you can distort the earnings of your business by living off the business profits, as we know a lot of small-business owners do.

Multiple of Sales

If you look at the stock value as a multiple of sales for a publicly traded company, you'll see that a lot of them have significant multiples—often two, three, four, and five times. We saw crazy numbers—even higher than that—back in the dot-com era.

There are some practical mathematical reasons to use this method, but you need to understand that a multiple of sales is a really a huge leap of faith because not all sales are created equal. It's probably the most inaccurate measure because you may have a different profit margin on every dollar of sales that runs through your business. It's possible they may all be the same, but it depends on the business. You will most likely see high multiples when it is an emerging market and people with money are willing to buy start-ups with hopes of building another Google or Microsoft.

In a lot of cases, though, here's what happens: If I have a $5 million business and every dollar of sales brings in the same profit margin, I may have penetrated all of the sales that will give me that profit margin at the $5 million level. If I want to grow to $20 million, my next dollar of sales will have to come in at a lower profit margin, which will dilute my existing sales. So it becomes a losing proposition at that point. A multiple of sales is probably the weakest of the multiple measures.

Discounted Projected Cash Flows

Another weak measure is using discounted projected cash flows. When it comes to projections, one of my former partners was always fond of saying, "You know, it's funny. We always make money on the spreadsheet, but at the end of the year it's not in the bank account."

This happens because everyone has the rosiest outlook for the future. This is largely why my firm has gotten more involved in doing forecasts. We want to add realism to the process rather than let our clients think of every possible good thing that could happen and avoid addressing the business cycles. For instance, you can't look at history and decide that a recurring dip in income at a particular point in time won't happen again this year.

Book Value or Liquidation Value

Book value and liquidation value are really two methods, but I'm combining them here. You use this method when there are net assets in the business but the business isn't profitable.

If I'm buying a company, I'm not going to give the current owners any benefit for their stream of profits or lack of profits. I'm going to offer to take over where they're at right now and pay for the money they have in the business. Then I'll try to build the business from there. In the current small-business environment, the most common valuation scenario is when there's a damaged business and its worth is based on its net assets.

If you're the owner, you might be willing to accept that offer. If you try to liquidate the business to get those values, you're going to incur more losses; therefore, you're actually going to get less than if you just handed the keys over to someone else. You're better off asking the buyer to pay for your receivables, pay off your payables and bank note, and then walk away happy to be free of an unsuccessful business venture.

When it comes to small businesses, book value is often a negative number. In this situation, you're actually paying someone to take over. Maybe you have other assets to protect and you want to get out from under the business. It is not uncommon for people in a small business to pay somebody to get them out of the hole. I see this all the time. But you'll rarely use a book value or liquidation value on the sale of an ongoing business, unless the market is just really horrible, there are no buyers, and it's a fire-sale situation.

EXAMPLES OF ECONOMIC VALUATIONS: THE MATH TELLS AN INTERESTING STORY

In the sections that follow, we will look at two companies, one at 10 percent pretax profit (Company A) and one at 15 percent pretax profit (Company B), each with two shareholders who own 50 percent. Pay attention to the drastic difference between the two companies in the outcome (both in value and distributions) at the end of five years. It really shows why profit matters not only to the ongoing health of your business, but also to the ultimate value of your business over time or in a sale.

Let's take a look at some of the basic math. In exhibit 9.1, Company A had $1 million in revenue in year one, $1.92 million in year two, $2.07 million in year three (it leveled off between years two and three); it jumped a little to $2.85 in year four, and then it hit $3 million in year five.

In chapter 2, we talked about what happens between $1 million and $5 million. The black hole, remember? The deepest abyss in the black hole is between $2 million and $4 million. Exhibit 9.1 takes a simple approach of 10 percent pretax profit across the board. If the company can manage to make 10 percent every year, that's great. But you might see some decline in earnings in the fourth and fifth years because they're in the middle of the black hole.

Exhibit 9.1: Company A: 10% Pretax Profit					
EBITDA History					
	Year 1	**Year 2**	**Year 3**	**Year 4**	**Year 5**
Revenue	$1,050,000	$1,920,000	$2,070,000	$2,850,000	$3,000,000
Net operating income (pretax profit)	105,000	192,000	207,000	285,000	300,000
% to income	*10.0%*	*10.0%*	*10.0%*	*10.0%*	*10.0%*
Tax distributions (40% on previous year)		42,000	76,800	82,800	114,000
Profit distributions (amounts above core capital target)		17,000	107,700	85,200	209,900
Total distributions	—	42,000	93,800	190,500	199,200
Equity at year end (assumes $50k to start)	155,000	305,000	418,200	512,700	613,500
Core capital target	157,500	288,000	310,500	427,500	450,000
Return on investment	68%	63%	49%	56%	49%

The business is showing 10 percent pretax profit each year, and tax distributions, which are 40 percent of the previous year's pretax profit, are listed separately to mimic the effect of taxation. You need to know when you are taking distributions for tax purposes and when distributions are profits after all taxes have been paid. Many companies are on the cash basis for taxes, so Company A pays taxes in the year following the profit, which is a good approximation of the actual taxes. In real life, taxes are calculated for each quarter. The timing may be slightly different, but this is fine for illustration purposes.

You take a profit distribution only when all of your taxes have been paid and you have money above your core capital target. Company A has two months of operating expenses as their core capital target.

Let's assume that Company A got started with $50,000 in capital. In the first year, they had 10 percent pretax profit, so that's $105,000 in net operating income (NOI). Their core capital at the end of the year is $155,000, which is the $50,000 they started with plus $105,000 in pretax profit.

They haven't made tax or profit distributions yet, so they are right at their core capital target of $157,500. Keep in mind that their core capital is $155,000, and they made $105,000. That's a 68 percent return on investment, which is pretty good.

In Year 2, Company A's revenue increased to $1.92 million, so at 10 percent pretax profit, that's $192,000 in NOI. They took a $42,000 tax distribution, which is 40 percent of the previous year's pretax profit ($105,000 x 0.40). They didn't take a profit distribution because their core capital at the end of the year was $305,000, and their core capital target was $288,000. They're not close enough to the target to take a profit distribution. The owners are getting a 63 percent return on investment, and they left it in the company. They're building core capital by paying taxes on their earnings. The owners would have to sell the company right now to get their return on investment. They might be tempted to take the money out because it seems like that is too much money to leave sitting there, but they resisted the urge. Remember that opportunities happen to those who have cash.

In Year 3, Company A had $2.07 million of revenue, $207,000 of pretax profit, and they paid $76,800 in taxes on the previous year's pretax profit ($192,000 x 0.40). Now they get to take a little profit distribution of $17,000, which is the difference between the previous year's year-end core capital and their core capital target for the previous year ($305,000 − $288,000 = $17,000). In Year 4, they took tax and profit distributions of $190,500 ($82,800 +$107,700). Overall, they got a little bit of a bump in the third year, but it's really in the fourth and fifth years that they got good profit distributions, and they made somewhere around a 50 percent return on their investment.

That's not based on the value of the company. That's based on the owners' investment in the company, which is the sum of the cash they put in plus the earnings they left in after they paid taxes, so the numbers are extremely valid.

Exhibit 9.2 calculates the fair market value (FMV) of Company A. The calculation begins in Year 5 with $792,000, which is the last three years of NOI. That gives them $613,500 of core capital. This adds up to a FMV before discounts of $1,405,500, which is the economic value of the complete business. In five years, Company A created a cash flow–generating asset worth $1.4 million that started with $50,000 in cash. It took a lot of hard work, and they had to defer the distribution of profits until they were stable, but the owners paid themselves a market-based wage the whole time.

Under IRS rules, businesses can typically take a 10 to 20 percent discount for lack of marketability and a 10 to 20 percent discount for lack of control. The lack of marketability discount applies when the transaction is for a company that is not publicly traded. The lack of control discount applies when stock is sold to someone who does not own a controlling interest (typically 51 percent). This is the general standard, but some people push the discounts a little higher or lower. As you can see, Company A can use a value of $899,520 if they want to sell shares to an existing employee or bring in someone else. Now they have to make a decision: do they want to sell at that value or at the higher value before discounts are applied?

Important Note: Resist the urge to give your stock to anyone. My experience with my own firm (and with clients) is that stock starts to have real value only when money changes hands. This may be in the form of a bonus or a true exchange of cash, but you are doing yourself an injustice to give it away unless it is for estate-planning purposes.

Exhibit 9.2: Company A FMV Calculation: 10% Pretax Profit

Valuation

Equity + 3 years EBITDA

If 3 years are not available, take the average of the years available times 3.

Value Calculation	Year 1	Year 2	Year 3	Year 4	Year 5
Average NOI	105,000	148,500	use last 3 yrs	use last 3 yrs	use last 3 yrs
x3	315,000	445,500	504,000	684,000	792,000
Equity	155,000	305,000	418,200	512,700	613,500
FMV before discounts	**470,000**	**750,500**	**922,200**	**1,196,700**	**1,405,500**
Discount for lack of marketability					
Percentage	20%	20%	20%	20%	20%
Amount	94,000	150,100	184,440	239,340	281,100
FMV before lack of control discount	376,000	600,400	737,760	957,360	1,124,400
Discount for lack of control					
Percentage	20%	20%	20%	20%	20%
Amount	75,200	120,080	147,552	191,472	224,880
FMV after applying discounts	**300,800**	**480,320**	**590,208**	**765,888**	**899,520**
Multiple of EBITDA				4.69	
Multiple of revenue				0.47	
Payback term at 100% sale				7%	
Tax				40%	
Years to repay				14.34	
Payment (3-year after-tax average)				158,400.00	

Company A can decide which number to use, but essentially the economic value is $1,405,500. The calculations at the bottom of exhibit 9.2 (based on year five) show that the multiple of EBITDA is 4.69. That's in line with the five times EBITDA number that people talk about. As a multiple of sales, though, it's only 0.47. The FMV is not one times sales because the company is not profitable enough at that level.

So here's the kicker. A buyer who looks at how long it would take to pay for Company A, will see that an average payment of $158,400 every year, is 60 percent of the average of Company A's NOI from the past three years. Remember, the IRS gets 40 percent, so the buyer can't fund a payment with 100 percent of pretax profit. To make a payment of exactly 60 percent, the buyer needs to be fully capitalized because there is no room to account for a year that doesn't act according to past history. If the buyer is not fully capitalized or has a drop in future earnings, it will be necessary to either go into debt or inject capital into the business to complete the purchase. For the buyer who purchases Company A for $1,405,000, it would produce $158,400 per year, and at 7 percent interest to finance it, it would take 14.34 years to pay it off.

Buyers often expect that the business will continue to run well without the previous owners, so a buyer who purchases Company A, expects a return on investment of 49 percent, as shown in exhibit 9.1. But the buyer's actual return will be somewhere between 20 and 30 percent. Buyer's need a higher return on investment than that because, more times than not, buyers want to grow the business and then sell it to someone else. Basically, when you buy a business, you have to pay attention to the net after-tax number. The value of the business over time cannot exceed that number unless you have some other reason to think it is worth more.

Public companies are known for buying businesses that are well above their own cash flow–generating capacity because they don't have a choice. They look at those of us who start businesses as if we're biofuel. They don't have the creativity to generate a lot of new business ideas or launch new markets, so they buy a business. Drug companies and tech companies do it all the time. That's just one of the reasons they're willing

Exhibit 9.3: Company B FMV Calculation: 15% Pretax Profit

EBITDA History

	Year 1	Year 2	Year 3	Year 4	Year 5
Revenue	$1,050,000	$1,920,000	$2,070,000	$2,850,000	$3,000,000
Net operating income (pretax profit)	157,500	288,000	310,500	427,500	450,000
% to income	15.0%	15.0%	15.0%	15.0%	15.0%
Tax Distributions (40% on previous year)		63,000	115,200	124,200	171,000
Profit distributions (amounts above core capital target)			160,500	174,050	192,800
Total Distributions	-	63,000	275,700	298,250	363,800
Core capital at year end (assumes $50k to start)	207,500	432,500	467,300	596,550	682,750
Core capital target	148,750	272,000	293,250	403,750	425,000
Return on Investment	76%	67%	66%	72%	66%

Valuation
Equity + last 3 years EBITDA
If 3 years are not available, take the average of the years available times 3.

Value Calculation

			use last 3 yrs	use last 3 yrs	use last 3 yrs
Average NOI	157,500	222,750	756,000	1,026,000	1,188,000
x3	472,500	668,250	467,300	596,550	682,750
Equity	207,500	432,500	1,223,300	1,622,550	1,870,750
FMV before discounts	680,000	1,100,750			
Discount for lack of marketability					
Percentage	20%	20%	20%	20%	20%
Amount	136,000	220,150	244,660	324,510	374,150
FMV before lack of control discount	544,000	880,600	978,640	1,298,040	1,496,600
Discount for lack of control					
Percentage	20%	20%	20%	20%	20%
Amount	108,800	176,120	195,728	259,608	299,320
FMV after applying discounts	435,200	704,480	782,912	1,038,432	1,197,280

Multiple of EBITDA	4.16
Multiple of Revenue	0.62
Payback term at 100% sale	7%
Tax	40%
Periods	11.84
Payment (3 year after tax average)	237,600.00

to pay a number that doesn't make cash flow–generating sense. In this regard, they need to buy from you more than you need to sell to them.

If I have a cash flow–generating business, I don't need to have a strategic buyer, or an industry buyer, or someone like that. There are people who can spot good businesses and are willing to pay cash for something that generates profits. And there are people who have been able to sacrifice profits today to build a business faster. But there are entrepreneur graveyards filled with people who bought businesses and couldn't make them work. Build your business on a strong foundation and have profitability all along the way. Then you can sell it to a strategic buyer who will look at it and say, "This is a great business!"

Now let's turn our attention to Company B, which makes 15 percent pretax profit.

Over a five-year period, Company B can take $527,350 of after-tax profit distributions. Under the 10 percent scenario, Company A was able to take $209,900. You can see that profitability matters, and it's huge in terms of the multiplication effect on the company's ability to make larger distributions and be more valuable!

50/50 Partner Buyout

Remember that in our examples, Companies A and B each have two shareholders who own 50 percent. Assume that one partner wants to buy out the other partner. Exhibit 9.4 shows how a five-year, 50 percent payout looks for Company A and their 10 percent pretax profit.

Exhibit 9.4:Company A: Five-Year, 50% Buyout				
You can buy half of the company from cash flows in 5 Years				
Value of company		$1,405,500.00		
(Use undiscounted value since it is 50% ownership)				

Purchase Value of 50%		$702,750.00		
Term in Years	5			
Interest Rate	7%			
Annual Payment		$171,394.19		
Sum of annual Payments		$856,970.93		
			-8.2%	% variance
			$(12,994.19)	Excess/(Shortfall)
Cash Flows available				any excess allows for slight funding of growth
Pretax Profit (3 yr avg)		$264,000.00		any shortfall has to be covered by capital, debt or growth
Tax Cost	40%	$105,600.00		
Net Available for Loan Payment		$158,400.00		
(Note: This assumes business is fully capitalized and does not need more working capital)				

If we value the business at $1,405,500, that means I have to pay $702,750 to buy my partner out. I'm going to pay that over five years. You can see that my three-year average of pretax profit is $264,000, and after taxes, I can use only $158,400 to make the payment. There's a shortfall of $12,994.19 between my annual payment ($171,394.19) and $158,400, which creates a variance of 8.2 percent (12,994.19 ÷ 158,400.00). I don't like to see more than a plus or minus 10 percent variance in either an overage or a shortfall.

If I really want to stay in the business, I'm not going to be able to take distributions over the next five years. The only time I can take distributions is when I increase my profitability from 10 percent to 15 percent. And getting rid of a partner might help me do that.

Exhibit 9.5 contrasts this scenario with Company B, which operates at 15 percent pretax profit.

Exhibit 9.5: Company B: Five-Year, 50% Buyout				
You can buy half of the company from cash flows in 5 years				
Value of company		$1,870,750.00		
(Use undiscounted value since it is 50% ownership)				
Purchase Value of 50%		$935,375.00		
Term in Years	5			
Interest Rate	7%			
Annual Payment		$228,129.26		
Sum of Annual Payments		$1,140,646.29		
			4.0%	% variance
			$9,470.74	Excess/(Shortfall)
Cash Flows available				any excess allows for slight funding of growth
Pretax Profit (3-yr avg)		$396,000.00		any shortfall has to be covered by capital, debt or growth
Tax Cost	40%	$158,400.00		
Net Available for Loan Payment		$237,600.00		
(Note: This assumes business is fully capitalized and does not need more working capital)				

Compare the variance for Companies A and B. With 15 percent pretax profit, the variance for Company B swings in the opposite direction. It has an *excess* of $9,470.74. But in this particular case, because the company is already at 15 percent profitability and I'm looking at buying out my partner, I'd probably be a little more cautious just to make sure this buyout is really going to work. I don't have as much room to grow the company's profitability when it's already at 15 percent. This might be a case where I want to talk about it a little bit. But there again, it's still very close to being a deal where I'm willing to take all my after-tax profits to buy out my partner.

COMPARING OUTCOMES AT 5 PERCENT, 10 PERCENT, AND 15 PERCENT

We looked in-depth at Company A, which gets 10 percent pretax profit, and Company B, which gets 15 percent pretax profit. We saw how their fair market values compare and what a 50/50 partner buyout would look like for each company. Now let's backtrack and see what happens with a company that gets only 5 percent pretax profit. Exhibit 9.6 shows the FMV calculations for this business.

Notice that this business is not even close to its core capital target until the fifth year. This is why you have to be profitable from the very beginning.

Take a look at exhibit 9.7, which shows the profit distributions for the company that gets 5 percent pretax profit, as well as Company A (10 percent pretax profit) and Company B (15 percent pretax profit) from our previous discussion.

In the data below the graph, you can see that if you make only 5 percent a year, it takes you five years to get to your core capital target, and you get no distributions. At the 10 percent level, you get meager distributions through the third year, and you get some decent distributions in Years 4 and 5. At the 15 percent level, you get good distributions, but even then you don't get distributions in the first two years.

Next, let's look at exhibit 9.8, which is a graph of the company values.

The 5 percent company started with a business that was slightly over $200,000 in value and ended with a business that was over $800,000 in value, but they don't have any cash flow to show for it. This assumes, of course, that the owners were taking market-based wages the whole time. If they had pushed a little harder and gotten to 10 percent, their business

Exhibit 9.6 : FMV Calculation at 5% Pretax Profit

EBITDA History

	Year 1	Year 2	Year 3	Year 4	Year 5
Revenue	$1,050,000	$1,920,000	$2,070,000	$2,850,000	$3,000,000
Net operating income (pretax profit)	52,500	96,000	103,500	142,500	150,000
% to income	**5.0%**	**5.0%**	**5.0%**	**5.0%**	**5.0%**
Tax distributions (40% on previous year)		21,000	38,400	41,400	57,000
Profit distributions (amounts above core capital target)		-	-	-	-
Total distributions	-	21,000	38,400	41,400	57,000
Core Capital at year end (assumes $50k to start)	102,500	177,500	242,600	343,700	436,700
Core capital target	166,250	304,000	327,750	451,250	475,000
Return on Investment	51%	54%	43%	41%	34%

Valuation

Equity + last 3 years EBITDA

If 3 years are not available, take the average of the years available times 3.

Value Calculation

	52,500	74,250	use last 3 yrs	use last 3 yrs	use last 3 yrs
Average NOI	52,500	74,250	use last 3 yrs	use last 3 yrs	use last 3 yrs
x3	157,500	222,750	252,000	342,000	396,000
Equity	102,500	177,500	242,600	343,700	436,700
FMV before discounts	**260,000**	**400,250**	**494,600**	**685,700**	**832,700**
Discount for lack of marketability					
Percentage	20%	20%	20%	20%	20%
Amount	52,000	80,050	98,920	137,140	166,540
FMV before lack of control discount	208,000	320,200	395,680	548,560	666,160
Discount for lack of control					
Percentage	20%	20%	20%	20%	20%
Amount	41,600	64,040	79,136	109,712	133,232
FMV after applying discounts	**166,400**	**256,160**	**316,544**	**438,848**	**532,928**

Multiple of EBITDA	5.55	
Multiple of revenue	0.28	
Payback term at 100% sale	7%	
Tax	40%	
Periods	19.68	
Payment (3 year after tax average)	79,200.00	

would have been valued at $1.4 million. And take a look at the value for 15 percent—over $1.8 million!

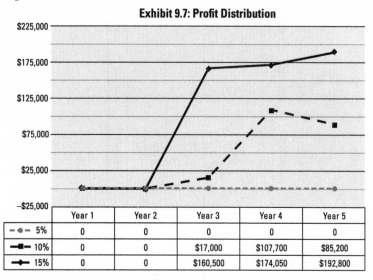

Exhibit 9.7: Profit Distribution

	Year 1	Year 2	Year 3	Year 4	Year 5
5%	0	0	0	0	0
10%	0	0	$17,000	$107,700	$85,200
15%	0	0	$160,500	$174,050	$192,800

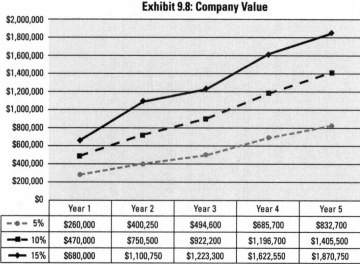

Exhibit 9.8: Company Value

	Year 1	Year 2	Year 3	Year 4	Year 5
5%	$260,000	$400,250	$494,600	$685,700	$832,700
10%	$470,000	$750,500	$922,200	$1,196,700	$1,405,500
15%	$680,000	$1,100,750	$1,223,300	$1,622,550	$1,870,750

Some of these exhibits have shown profit distributions, so let's take a look at the graph in exhibit 9.9, which shows value plus distributions.

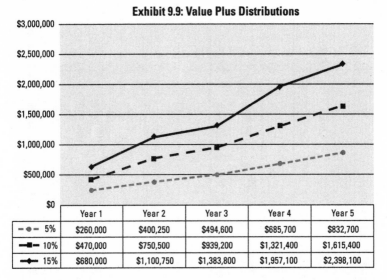

Exhibit 9.9: Value Plus Distributions

	Year 1	Year 2	Year 3	Year 4	Year 5
● 5%	$260,000	$400,250	$494,600	$685,700	$832,700
■ 10%	$470,000	$750,500	$939,200	$1,321,400	$1,615,400
◆ 15%	$680,000	$1,100,750	$1,383,800	$1,957,100	$2,398,100

You can see that the value of the 5 percent business is still $832,700, but the value of the 15 percent business is almost $2.4 million—three times as much! Also, notice the slope of the 15 percent curve. It rises faster than the other curves. Obviously, you have to start pushing and get your business to 15 percent profitability.

EXAMPLE: SALE OF STOCK TO A KEY EMPLOYEE

Next, let's look at an example of a shareholder sale in exhibit 9.10.

Let's say I have a million shares of stock in the company, and I sell 10 percent of the stock to an employee in Year 1 based on that value. I sell the stock at the discounted value of $43,520. Keep in mind that I either have to withhold taxes from that or the employee has to pay the taxes. Remember, if you can't get buyers to pay cash or justify it as part of their market-based wage, you are just being charitable. This is the same concept we discussed in chapter 7 when we were trying to get Patrick to buy stock instead of taking the net pay from his bonus.

If the employee holds their stock until the company is sold, they're going to get at least the FMV before discounts because everybody goes

Exhibit 9.10: FMV Calculation—15% Shareholder Example

EBITDA History

	20X1	20X2	20X3	20X4	20X5
Revenue	$1,050,000	$1,920,000	$2,070,000	$2,850,000	$3,000,000
Net operating income	157,500	288,000	310,500	427,500	450,000
% to income	*15.0%*	*15.0%*	*15.0%*	*15.0%*	*15.0%*
Equity at year end (assumes $50k to start)	207,500	432,500	467,300	596,550	682,750
Valuation					
Value Calculation					
Average NOI	157,500	222,750	use last 3 yrs	use last 3 yrs	use last 3 yrs
x3	472,500	668,250	756,000	1,026,000	1,188,000
Equity	207,500	432,500	467,300	596,550	682,750
FMV before discounts	*680,000*	*1,100,750*	*1,223,300*	*1,622,550*	*1,870,750*
FMV after applying discounts	*435,200*	*704,480*	*782,912*	*1,038,432*	*1,197,280*

Multiple of EBITDA	4.16	
Multiple of sales	0.62	
Payback term at 100% sale	7%	
Tax	40%	
Years to repay	11.84	
Payment (3-year after-tax average)	237,600.00	

Shareholder sale example	10%	10%	10%	10%	10%
Number of shares outstanding	1,000,000	1,000,000	1,000,000	1,000,000	1,000,000
Shares sold	100,000	100,000	100,000	100,000	100,000
Price per share internal	$0.4352	$0.7045	$0.7829	$1.0384	$1.1973
Price per share external	$0.6800	$1.1008	$1.2233	$1.6226	$1.8708
Shareholder purchase	43,520				
Internal sale value by year (after discounts)	$43,520	$70,448	$78,291	$103,843	$119,728
External value by year (before discounts)	$68,000	$110,075	$122,330	$162,255	$187,075

out as co-shareholders. But if the employee leaves before anybody else, you will owe them for their stock, and you will have to buy it back. I believe that the buy-sell of a less-than-50-percent shareholder has to be based on the FMV *after* the discounts are applied.

I also believe that the buy-sell needs to occur over a five-year payout period. One of the best examples of all time is Outback Steakhouse. I was told at a conference (by the CEO at that time) that store managers who sell their 10 percent ownership of their store have to wait two years, and then they're paid out over a five-year period based on a formula.

You can come up with all kinds of formulas, but if you have a 10 percent shareholder, you can say, "If you want to leave early, we owe you for your stock because you paid for it and it's worth whatever the math says it's worth." In this example, the employee bought the stock for $43,520, and the internal value in Year 5 is actually $119,728. If the 10 percent owner leaves before the whole company is sold, I contend they should never get more than the discounted value.

If the whole company is sold in the fifth year, you'll pay the employee $187,075 for the stock they bought for $43,520, assuming the company sells for at least its economic value (the employee will get whatever their ratable share is in an overall sale). Only in the total sale of the company does the minority shareholder get an undiscounted value.

These deals fail when the cash flow does not match the promises you've made and it forces you into selling the complete business to follow through on the promise! You should never structure a shareholder transaction promise that requires the sale of the business to complete the transaction. This is what I refer to as the *last one out loses* scenario.

When I do this analysis with someone, I make sure they understand they're never going to buy out a partner, and both partners have to decide to sell the business. That's the only way you're going to get out. Also realize there are times in the market when there's no appetite to buy a complete business. This is especially true for a business that's worth less than $5 million.

There is a fragmented market of willing buyers for businesses that are valued at less than $10 million, and the market gets more fragmented as the businesses get smaller. There are plenty of times when there aren't buyers at higher dollar levels, either, but even in today's economy there's plenty of money available to buy businesses. Now more than ever, buyers are focusing on businesses that have cash-flow-generating capacity.

Chapter 9 Keys

1. Knowing the economic value of your business gives you a baseline to make decisions about either selling or keeping your business.

2. The fair market value of your business sets the baseline for decisions in 50/50 shareholder deals. Generally, if you can buy out your partner for less than the economic value, you should take the deal. If your partner is offering more than the economic value, consider selling.

3. Beware of agreeing to a deal that does not have a chance of succeeding. Even if you have already been paid, the buyer can come back and seek damages from any possible overstatements.

4. The five elements of value lead to a profitable business that is well capitalized.

5. Beware of using rule-of-thumb methods to calculate the value of your business because they can introduce both positive and negative distortions.

6. Profit really matters in the value of a business and in profit distributions. Position your business so you can be patient, and keep profits in the business until you are debt free.

7. Set realistic expectations whenever you offer stock to key employees. Do the math on what your stock is really worth

today and what you expect it to be worth if the employee leaves before the company is sold.

8. Do not give away your stock! Your cash is cheap; your stock is expensive!

CHAPTER 10

SKIP THE BUDGET, LEARN TO FORECAST

A budget is a license to spend; a forecast is your road map to profitability.

I had a partner who once observed that we always make a profit on the forecast. The problem was we did not follow through on what we said we'd do, which would have led to a *real* profit when the year was over. We had to learn (just like all of our clients) that the walk is more important than the talk.

To make forecasts work, they have to go hand in hand with execution. In frustration, entrepreneurs resort to budgets when their forecasts do not come true. When I speak to entrepreneurs, the most common thing I hear is: "I need a budget." My response is always, "No, you don't. You need a business model and a forecast you are willing to act on."

Budgets are, essentially, a license to spend. They're not a roadmap to making money. They're not flexible when it comes to changing business conditions. I can have a budget for rent because that doesn't change. But I can't have a budget for office supplies because I should buy office supplies only when it's absolutely necessary in order to run the business. If you budget that number, you'll have to make someone the office supplies police. Someone would have to make sure you buy pens that are 20 percent cheaper. Likewise, you can't cut your kitchen supplies enough to turn yourself into a profitable business. I had a partner who, whenever things got tight, started counting how many soft drinks one of our staff members was consuming. That's just not sending the right message about your culture. No, you don't want to be wasteful. If I see anyone truly taking advantage of the kitchen supplies, that's really just a teachable moment for me to counsel that person or suggest a career change.

Budgeting is one of those things that can make you keep your head down when you actually need to keep your head up to see what's coming at you. Instead, spend 25 percent of your effort looking at what has happened and 75 percent of your effort looking at numbers and thinking about what you want to *make* happen.

I began thinking differently about this when I had a two-day tour at Springfield ReManufacturing, a Jack Stack company that I mentioned in an earlier chapter. I was blown away by the people in that company. Machine operators, clerks, shippers—people who had never taken an accounting class in college—could explain a balance sheet, a P&L, and a cash flow statement better than any accountant I'd ever met in my life. Not only that, they updated their current month and remainder-of-the-year forecasts *each week*! At that point, it dawned on me that I was making this too hard.

Springfield ReManufacturing had a simple process. They would draw up a plan for the entire year, but more importantly, they would forecast for the entire year. The plan was drawn up once, but the forecasts were updated each month as actual results became known and better information was available to forecast expectations for the remainder of the year. When they began the month of April, they would know the actual numbers from January through March. Then they would make a weekly projection of what they thought was going to happen in April. Then they projected data on a month-to-month basis so they had a forecast for the rest of the year. They knew, based on three months of actual data and nine months of forecasts, where they thought they were going to be by the end of the year.

It's easier to keep up with this than it seems. I draw up a plan at the beginning of the year that says what I expect that year. Here's the revenue. Here's the cost. Here's my expected pretax profit. Here's how I'm going to use the cash. When the annual plan is done, it goes in a drawer, and I may look back at it only once a quarter—or maybe not at all. The more relevant question is this: What have I actually done to this point, and what do I think is going to happen over the rest of the year? You start to realize you don't have to keep reinventing the wheel and wondering what's going to happen next. You're much more in the flow of things because you're constantly looking at what has happened and what's *going* to happen. You start to get a sense of the momentum of your business and where it's going to take you.

You're going to understand that there are certain things you can't change right away. It's much like the Exxon Valdez. They knew several hours in advance that they were going to run ashore in Alaska and create an oil spill. But a large and heavy barge can't turn on a dime. Most businesses are very similar. You'll learn what your turn rate is, and you'll learn the answers to these questions: How long does it take for you to make a decision? Can you trim labor based on hourly metrics like the Outbacks and Starbucks of the world, or do you rely on weekly or monthly metrics? You'll refine the answers until you get it down to the smallest possible time increment.

That may sound like a lot of work, but you don't have to fill in every detail on the P&L or the balance sheet. Keep it simple, and answer questions such as "What's my revenue? What's my cost of goods sold? What's my labor? What are my operating expenses?" When you get the data at those high levels, you'll see that the numbers don't move around as much as you thought they would. You'll understand that the economic engine of your business is pretax profit.

In a previous chapter, I talked about cash being the critical number for Jack Stack's first year in business. He wanted to know what the cash balance was so he'd never run out. Once you're fully capitalized, cash isn't usually your critical number. After the first year, you think more along the lines of how profitable you can be and if you can set a record. This is when you start to look at your business metrics. Don't look at the metrics of other companies; set your own metrics and break your own records. Keep stretching until you find the edges to improve your performance.

At this point I want to give you a word of caution. There are a lot of people who sell very expensive, very detail-oriented cash-flow projection systems that allow you to create massive spreadsheets. Don't buy or create a system that requires far more effort to update than the value you get from of it. If you spend all of your effort updating the system, you'll spend very little time analyzing the data. If a complex model is not talking to you, don't pay for it. Sometimes I use a complex model for a client when I need to explain things clearly, but if the client doesn't get any benefit from it, I stop using it.

THE BASICS OF A SIMPLE FORECAST MODEL

You already know you have to keep forecasting simple, so first let's try to understand one month. If you can understand how the data from a profit-and-loss statement for one month turns into cash, then you can start expanding it into multiple months.

Take a look at the simple cash-flow model in exhibit 10.1 (a copy of the model is available at www.seeingbeyondnumbers.com).

Interpreting the Data

In exhibit 10.1, the first two columns represent two months of actual data. The next three columns represent forecast data. In the forecast columns, the shaded areas represent the fields you have to input to drive the model calculations.

You can see the basic elements I've talked about: revenue, cost of goods sold (in this example, there's no labor component in cost of goods sold), and operating expenses. The five most common operating expenses are salaries, marketing, facilities, payroll taxes and benefits, and other operating expenses. The result of all that activity is your net operating income.

In addition to these amounts, you want to see two critical percentages: gross profit and net operating income (pretax profit) as a percentage of revenue. You can lower your gross profit and potentially improve your pretax profit by making changes, such as sales volume or employee salaries, but pretax profit as a percentage of revenue is the most important number.

The Road Map from Profit to Cash

In Month 1, there's $8,000 of net operating income, but that isn't cash. There are some essential elements that will lead you to the cash number. The first thing you look at is accounts receivable (A/R). If you get paid immediately upon performance or sale or whatever you do, then A/R is irrelevant, but the vast majority of businesses have A/R.

In exhibit 10.1, you have a beginning accounts receivable balance of $95,000 coming into the year. It ends with a $110,000 balance, which means your receivables went up. Subtract the beginning balance from the ending balance to get the net change, or the cash impact, which is $15,000. It's one of those times where growth actually *used* cash. You need to understand that when it comes to cash flow, a rise in accounts receivable uses cash.

Now let's look at payables. The beginning balance is $20,000, and the ending balance is $15,000, so your payables went down. That means you had to *use* cash to lower your payables, so that results in a net change of $5,000 of cash used.

Another major component of the forecast is debt. You started the month with a debt of $50,000 and ended the month with a debt of $65,000, so you created $15,000 of cash through debt sources.

Everybody forgets to look at shareholder's equity. There are two things that can happen there. You can either put money in (add it) or you can take money out (subtract it). In exhibit 10.1, you took out $5,000 as a distribution, so the total net change in cash is minus $2,000.

Sometimes there are two other elements, but they're not shown in exhibit 10.1. If you had inventory or fixed asset purchases and sales, you'd handle that the same way as shown in the A/R example.

The next item in the exhibit is the total net change in cash. When you look at the cash flow forecast for the next month, you can see that

Exhibit 10.1: Simple Cash Flow Model

	Actual			Forecast	
	Month 1	Month 2	Month 3	Month 4	Month 5
Revenue	100,000.00	110,000.00	105,000.00	120,000.00	130,000.00
Cost of Goods Sold	60,000.00	63,800.00	59,850.00	66,000.00	70,200.00
Gross Profit	40,000.00	46,200.00	45,150.00	54,000.00	59,800.00
as % of Revenue	40%	42%	43%	45%	46%
Operating Expenses					
Labor - All	15,000.00	15,000.00	18,000.00	20,000.00	21,000.00
Marketing	1,500.00	1,500.00	2,000.00	2,000.00	2,000.00
Facilities	5,000.00	5,000.00	5,000.00	5,000.00	5,000.00
Payroll taxes & benefits	3,000.00	3,000.00	3,600.00	4,000.00	4,200.00
Other operating expenses	7,500.00	7,500.00	7,000.00	7,000.00	7,000.00
Total Operating Expenses	32,000.00	32,000.00	35,600.00	38,000.00	39,200.00
(Pretax Profit)	8,000.00	14,200.00	9,550.00	16,000.00	20,600.00
as % to Revenue	8.00%	12.91%	9.10%	13.33%	15.85%
Cash flow adjustments:					
Accounts receivable:					
Beginning (add)	95,000.00	110,000.00	100,000.00	107,500.00	112,500.00
Ending (subtract)	110,000.00	100,000.00	107,500.00	112,500.00	125,000.00
Net change	(15,000.00)	10,000.00	(7,500.00)	(5,000.00)	(12,500.00)

	Col 1	Col 2	Col 3	Col 4	Col 5
Payables					
Beginning (subtract)	20,000.00	15,000.00	15,000.00	15,000.00	15,000.00
Ending (add)	15,000.00	20,000.00	20,000.00	20,000.00	20,000.00
Net change	(5,000.00)	5,000.00	5,000.00	5,000.00	5,000.00
Debt					
Beginning (subtract)	50,000.00	65,000.00	35,000.00	30,000.00	25,000.00
Ending (add)	65,000.00	35,000.00	30,000.00	25,000.00	20,000.00
Net change	15,000.00	(30,000.00)	(5,000.00)	(5,000.00)	(5,000.00)
Equity changes					
Capital injected (add)	-	-	-	-	-
Distributions (subtract)	5,000.00	-	-	-	18,460.00
Net change	(5,000.00)	-	-	-	(18,460.00)
Total net change in cash	(2,000.00)	(800.00)	2,050.00	11,000.00	(10,360.00)
Cash					
Beginning	25,000.00	23,000.00	22,200.00	24,250.00	35,250.00
Ending	23,000.00	22,200.00	24,250.00	35,250.00	24,890.00
Labor efficiency MTD	2.67	3.08	2.51	2.70	2.85
Labor efficiency YTD	2.67	2.87	2.74	2.73	2.75
Accounts receivable DSO	33.46	27.65	30.00	30.00	30.00
Core Capital	(42,000.00)	(12,800.00)	(5,750.00)	10,250.00	4,890.00
Core Capital Target (w/o COGS)	64,000.00	64,000.00	71,200.00	76,000.00	78,400.00
Core Capital Target (with COGS)	184,000.00	191,600.00	190,900.00	208,000.00	218,800.00

the beginning number for each of the cash flow adjustment items is the same as the previous month's ending number, so all you have to do to forecast the next month's total net change in cash is to estimate what will happen in that month.

For instance, if you know that A/R is too high, you have a target to shoot for. You can't just hope that A/R goes down. Hope is not a strategy. You have to start making tougher negotiations and maybe stop being too nice a lot of the time. Try this technique: Every time you're in a business relationship and think you're being extra nice, look at a picture of your spouse and your children sitting at a table with no food on it. Then decide how nice you really want to be. It's business, and while it's important to be nice, it's important to develop solid relationships with people who pay their bills.

Driving the Forecast

Now you have all the elements you need for your forecast, so you can continue to build it across your spreadsheet for all of the months. You can forecast by quarter, per six months, or possibly even per year. As time goes by and you have actual numbers, you can go back and drop in the real data. Then you do what Springfield ReManufacturing does, and you reforecast the future. This task will take less than an hour each month, and when you become really adept at it, it may take only fifteen minutes.

You can drive your gross profit calculation by forecasting your sales and your gross profit percentage. The model calculates cost of goods sold and gross profit dollars by inputting the target gross profit percentage. All of your operating expense categories are easy to predict. History will tell you what the future is going to be unless you decide to add or eliminate a cost. Labor should be the easiest to predict since it is a function of your staff structure.

Predicting the cash flow section is where most people go wrong. Your A/R is driven by your manual input of days sales outstanding (DSO), which I'll explain in a moment. You can easily input your payables based on your past history with your vendors. Debt is an input cell based on either available cash or fixed payment requirements. Capital injections and distributions are input cells, too. I hope I have convinced you that you should take only tax distributions until you hit your core capital target. You can see in Month 5 that the distribution amount is 40 percent of the three previous months' pretax profit.

You can structure this forecast so the data easily comes straight out of your accounting system. If you think it's difficult, you should visit Springfield ReManufacturing and be humbled by factory workers who will run circles around you when it comes to understanding this data.

Key Metrics

Now that your forecast is complete, you can create those metrics we talked about earlier. It's important to understand that a metric is more about *movement* than it is about the number itself. If you take a specific metric and compare it to another company, you need to make sure it's calculated the same way and it means the same thing for your industry. It is more important to set and exceed your own company goals.

The first thing I want you to focus on is labor efficiency. This represents the productivity of your employees. There will be some high months and some low months. Exhibit 10.1 calculates labor efficiency on a month-to-date and year-to-date basis so you can identify trends.

Next is accounts receivable DSO, which is your A/R divided by your average daily sales. Here's the simple calculation: Take this month's revenue, multiply it by 12, then divide it by 365, and that gives you your average daily sales. To get your DSO, take your end-of-month A/R balance and divide it by your average daily sales. Use a little caution here because this metric isn't always calculated the same way. If you're using annual data, it's going to be distorted if the business goes through seasonal or other cycles. I prefer to look at the last two months of revenue to come up with the average daily sales number. A/R generally falls over a two-month period, so I can forecast the average daily sales either too high or too low, depending on whether I'm in a high season or a low season. If I'm in the second month of the year, I'm going to create my daily sales number by averaging the two months. Whatever method you choose, use it consistently.

Another critical metric is the measurement of core capital. Remember that your core capital target is two months of operating expenses in cash with nothing drawn on your line of credit. Exhibit 10.1 shows that in Month 1, if you just count operating expenses, your core capital target is $64,000 ($32,000 x 2). If you include Cost of Goods Sold and Operating Expenses, your core capital target is $184,000 (60,000 + 32,000 = 92,000, then double that sum).

You should choose one of these calculations. Let's say I have trade support for my cost of goods sold, which means that the cost of goods sold number is a subcontractor and that subcontractor is willing to be paid when I get paid. If this is the case, then I do not include it in my core capital target calculation. But if I have to pay for that cost of goods sold before I get paid, then I have to include it.

In exhibit 10.1, your core capital target in Month 1 is negative $42,000. That's the ending cash balance of $23,000 minus the ending debt balance of $65,000. Remember, you're not fully capitalized until you're out of debt and you have cash in the bank to cover two months of your operating expenses. You can't take distributions—except for taxes—until you've hit your core capital target.

You've seen a lot of examples in this book where it doesn't take long to get to your core capital target, but you do have to go through this period of building capital. Then you'll have the cash resources to react to opportunities that cross your path. If you have debt, you won't even find the opportunities. The people with cash always win.

Exhibit 10.1 is a simplified forecast where we combined the P&L with the cash flow so you can see how to fix it. So you should be able to come back to an expected cash number at the end of the statement. When you understand this forecast, you're ready to take a look at a more formal, complex model.

COMPLEX CASH FLOW MODEL

As your business matures, you will likely need to move to a more complex cash flow model. The model I create for my clients still retains its simplicity of rolling up to limited lines of data, but it includes a more detailed forecast and presentation of the balance sheet and cash flow statement that most bankers and investors like to see. You can go to my website to download an example of this model (www.seeingbeyond-numbers.com).

There are two real advantages of the advanced model. First, you can look at data that covers a much longer period of time. Second, you can do a rolling-twelve calculation for your P&L and calculate your key metrics. When you display the rolling-twelve data either graphically, as shown in exhibit 10.2, or as a grid of numbers, you can scan the numbers across time and see the real movement of the data.

When you look at rolling-twelve data in a graph, you see some really interesting trends. I don't much care about revenue growth; I care about gross profit growth. Sometimes I remove revenue from the graph if there's a really low gross margin percentage, but if I can get it all on the same graph, it's good to have both. So typically, I want to graph revenue and gross profit on a rolling twelve basis.

Exhibit 10.2 shows adjusted labor and adjusted pretax profit. A lot of the people I work with have historical data that's distorted. Can you guess why? It's because they haven't been taking a market-based wage and they've been including distributions that really should have been salary. I do a calculation to show what the adjusted labor should be. Obviously, the adjusted labor creates adjusted pretax profit, and both appear in the graph. Adjusted pretax profit is the actual pretax profit minus the distributions that should have been taken out of the salary total because it should have been a salary expense. If you show $100,000 of profit but take $110,000 in distributions that should have been salary, you really had a $10,000 loss. That's significant because it means your

Exhibit 10.2: Rolling-Twelve Graph

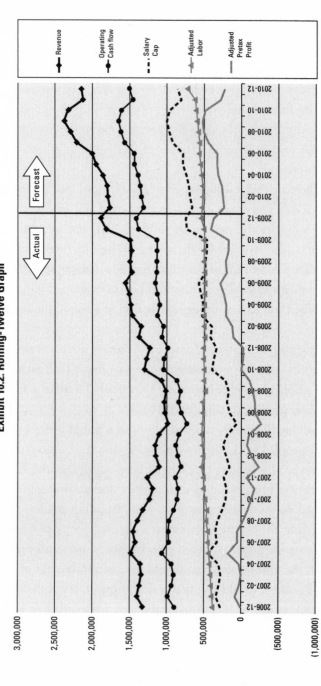

economic engine is broken. Your business needs to be able to pay you a market-based wage and still make a profit.

Another metric that's critical to monitor is the salary cap. As you look across the graph, any time that the salary cap is below the adjusted labor line, you had a lack of profitability. As we've talked about in previous chapters, you have two choices: cut salaries to meet the salary cap or don't spend additional money on salaries until your gross profit has increased. Usually, it's a blend of the two. Until your salary cap line is above the actual labor line, your business is underperforming.

The sooner people see changes happening, the better they understand the causes, and the faster they respond. A quick response makes it less likely that you'll have a multiple-month decline. Otherwise, you'll end up against the wall and have no choice but to change. You should make changes before you run out of resources, and that's what these forecasts are designed to help you with. If your forecasts don't prompt you to make changes before disaster strikes, you've wasted your time and effort.

In most businesses, there's a significant disconnect between pretax profit and the *actual cash flow*. I use a full forecast model to help my clients evaluate their business strategy. The model is built around a full presentation of profit and loss, the projected balance sheet, and the projected cash flow statement (including both historical and forecast data) and a dashboard summary to recap key metrics, so it shows the relationship between pretax profit and actual cash flow. My staff can take a month of a client's information and update this model in less than an hour. It looks complex, but we've found ways to make it very efficient and cost effective. We don't want to spend so much time updating the model that we don't have time to look at it and understand what the data is saying.

When the dashboard is complete, we can answer questions like: Where do you stand on profitability? How close are you to your sales targets? What are your operating expenses? How do you fare on your salary cap? How are your collections or DSO and receivables? Where are you in regard to your core capital target? Do you understand the tax implications of the profit?

Exhibit 10.3: Dashboard			
Sample Company as of (date)			
Grading Legend	Great		
	OK		
	Caution		**Rolling 12 Actual**
		Target	
Profitability	OK	15%	18.20%
Sales	Great	$3,000,000.00	$2,820,482.76
Overhead	Great	$1,200,000.00	$1,158,130.79
Salary Cap	Great	$668,574.92	$595,240.13
A/R DSO	Great	40.00	36.00
Core Capital Target	OK	$215,895.44	$(81,072.28)
Tax Implications	OK		
Commentary			
Profitability	OK		

Adjusted net income as % of revenue is at 18.2% Rolling 12 through the next year

Q2 profitability was great but remainder of the year looks weaker than history

Sales	Great		

How will the rest of the year fare?

Status of sales people hired?

Overhead	Great		

Nothing outside of what had been planned

Salary Cap	Great		

Salary Cap (R12) is better than target for 10% and 15% pre-tax profit level.

A/R DSO	Great		

Nothing out of the ordinary from DSO

Core Capital Target	Caution		

Really close to financing limits on the work in the first half of the year

Need to get debt down and be better prepared to self finance next opportunity

Tax Implications	OK		

Tax issues will be known at Q3 when receivables come in

Hold on to cash and no distributions until taxes are set aside and debt is gone.

Exhibit 10.3 is an example of the dashboard tab in the spreadsheet. It shows how we combine both data and comments because there are times when it is important to note when we see a troubling trend. We also use green (Great), yellow (OK), and red (Caution) to add visibility to the grading legend.

You can take a simple or a sophisticated, complex approach to your forecasting models. Either way, as you work more with your forecasting models, you'll begin to create your road map to profitability.

Chapter 10 Keys

1. Use regularly updated forecasts instead of budgets. Budgets are a license to spend, forecasts are a license to make profit.

2. Keep your forecast at high level. Detailed forecasts do not encourage regular updating, and they'll take so much time to maintain that you won't have time to evaluate them.

3. Evaluate your key metrics to understand the movement of your data.

4. Your forecast must connect your P&L to your balance sheet. Keep your eye on how your cash lags your profitability.

5. Rolling-twelve data gives you the best sense of mega trends in the business. The sooner you detect a change, the sooner you can fix it.

SUMMARY

THE FOURTEEN-YEAR OVERNIGHT SUCCESS

A few years ago I picked up a new client who had a good business but struggled to get out of debt and be consistently profitable. I told him when we started that I thought he had a good business model and that within eighteen months he would see a world of difference. He took my concepts to heart and the business began to flourish.

He quickly hit his profit target once he understood how his habit of taking distributions was distorting his pretax profit. Being a sports guy, he easily grasped the concept of the salary cap and started managing labor costs for maximum productivity. Once profits started to roll in, he quickly got the business out of debt and started building toward his core capital target.

Then came the moment of truth: it was time to pay taxes. He owed more in taxes than ever. He paused, then he realized he had the cash to pay it and there was no need to spend his profits at the end of the year to avoid taxes.

The next year brought greater profitability, and he was able to distribute enough after-tax profit to get out of debt personally and start building his personal wealth. In his own words, he became a "fourteen-year overnight success." The potential was there all along, he just needed a better game plan to harness the power of the business model he had conceived.

The market is a cruel place that sometimes rewards the foolish and punishes the brilliant. The difference, though, is that the foolish eventually lose their good fortune (unless they wise up) and the brilliant find a way to survive and make it work—even if it takes fourteen years.

I cannot pick your business model for you, but in this book I have outlined the keys to success that my clients have used to build successful businesses and to grow their personal wealth. If you do not have the time to read the whole book, these are the key concepts I want you to take away and apply to your business:

1. Get owner compensation right and stop playing games with distributions. This concept affects everything in your business, so that's why I list it first.

2. The new breakeven is 10 percent pretax profit. If you allow your business to drop below 10 percent profitability, you are waiting too long to make the necessary changes to keep it healthy.

3. Labor efficiency is the key to profitability. Nothing happens in business without human effort. It is not about how many people you have, if they are highly paid, or if they're lower-wage, entry-level employees. It is about how much productivity (gross profit) you get for every dollar of labor.

4. The four forces of cash flow—paying your taxes, repaying debt, reaching your core capital target, and taking profit distributions—are the physics of business. You can defy them temporarily, but they will eventually win.

5. Pay your taxes (or set aside the cash to pay them) as you go. Don't let the IRS be your lender.

6. Build a team culture around labor productivity. Communicate your expectations to your team and hold them accountable. Do not expect to use incentive pay as a substitute for leadership and management.

7. If you are undercapitalized, look for the capital source that fits you and your business model. The foundational concepts I

have laid out to build your business will also help you and your investors play nicely with each other.

8. Establish an effective reporting system and stick to it! Looking at too much data too often can be just as bad as looking at no data at all.

9. Understand the economic value of your business so you have a baseline for equity decisions.

10. Spend 75 percent of your time looking ahead at what you plan to make happen and 25 percent of your time reviewing actual performance. Keep your forecasts simple so they do not become a burden to update.

These concepts will help you become a world-class entrepreneur. Visit my website at www.seeingbeyondnumbers.com to share your story and find more resources to help you on your journey.

ABOUT THE AUTHORS

GREG CRABTREE

Greg Crabtree used his entrepreneurial skills to develop a CPA firm, Crabtree, Rowe & Berger, PC, which is dedicated to helping entrepreneurs build the economic engine of their business. Greg challenges entrepreneurs to take responsibility for understanding their own data, identifying the key drivers in their business, and simplifying key data reporting.

Greg started his firm in 1986 after spending five years with a regional accounting firm and three years as VP of operations/controller for a local bank. Greg's banking experience contributed to his firm's focus on financial modeling and data-driven decision analysis while still providing traditional tax and financial statement services. From their office in Huntsville, Alabama, the firm's twenty-one employees serve clients all over the United States.

In addition to serving as the firm's CEO, Greg leads the business consulting team. They help both mature and emerging businesses develop strategies, systems, and organizational structures to meet financial goals and priorities. This process allows clients to align their financial goals with their profit model and their core business values. Greg and his team structure monitoring programs to help their clients stay on track, and they provide their clients with financial analyses to verify if changes have a positive financial impact. Rather than focus on one particular industry, Greg and his team search for best practices among their clients and other business sources and share them across industries.

Greg serves as board member to several companies as well as the ALS Association of Alabama, Boys and Girls Clubs of North Alabama, and the Atlanta chapter of The Entrepreneurs' Organization. From 2006 to 2009, Greg was named to the Entrepreneurs' Organization Global

Board, and he served as chair of the Standing Finance Committee and was board liaison to the Strategic Alliances Committee and the Technology Committee. He enjoys invitations to many speaking engagements as a result of his expertise and numerous experiences with his own clients.

Greg and his wife Debbie have four children. Greg is an avid golfer and enjoys playing historic golf courses whenever his travel plans permit.

BEVERLY BLAIR HARZOG

Beverly Blair Harzog is a consumer advocate and credit card expert for Credit.com. She is coauthor of *The Complete Idiot's Guide to Person-to-Person Lending* (Alpha/Penguin, 2009). She is also an award-winning financial journalist, and her byline has appeared in CNNMoney.com, FoxBusiness.com, *Good Housekeeping*, Bankrate.com, *Bottom Line Wealth*, MSNMoney.com, CreditCards.com, *Wealth Manager*, *Your Business*, *Better Homes and Gardens*, and more.

In addition, Beverly has an MBA and is a former CPA. She lives with her husband and their two children in Johns Creek, Georgia, a northern suburb of Atlanta. Follow her on Twitter @BeverlyHarzog or visit her website at www.beverlyharzog.com.